MW00611805
To Reach the Top!

To Jenny the Kid!

For

Kitae

and

Denise Elizabeth

SELF RECRUITER®

Changing the Rules:

How to Be Your Own Recruiter & Ride the Economic Crisis to Your Next Career Challenge.

John Crant

Self-Recruiter®
Changing the Rules: How to Be Your Own Recruiter &
Ride the Economic Crisis to Your Next Career Challenge.

Published by Provident Resource, Inc.

For information, contact the publisher:
Provident Resource, Inc.
572 Grand Street, Suite G-705
New York, NY 10002

More information is available at: www.SelfRecruiter.com

Printed in the United States of America
First Printing: February 2009

Library of Congress Control Number: 2009921654

Publishers Catalogue-in-Publications Data

Crant, John
Self-Recruiter Changing the Rules: How to Be Your Own Recruiter &
Ride the Economic Crisis to Your Next Career Challenge./John Crant - 1st ed.
p. cm.
Includes index.
ISBN 978-0-9819592-0-7

1. Job Hunting. 2. Job Hunting - Psychological Aspects 3. Interviewing 4. Assertiveness (Psychology). 5. Persuasion (Psychology) I. Title. Self-Recruiter® Changing the Rules: How to Be Your Own Recruiter & Ride the Economic Crisis to Your Next Career Challenge.

HF5382.7.B472 2009
650.14-DC22

2009023660
PCIP

Provident Resource books are available at special discounts when purchased in bulk quantities for businesses, associations, institutions or sales promotions.
Please call our Special Markets Sales Department at 212-372-3093.

ISBN 978-0-9819592-0-7

Editor: John Crant
Interior Text Design: Daniel Kitae Um (www.danielkitaeum.com)
Cover / Jacket Design: Daniel Kitae Um (www.danielkitaeum.com)
Self-Recruiter Logo Design: Daniel Kitae Um (www.danielkitaeum.com)

More information is available at: www.SelfRecruiter.com

TABLE OF CONTENTS

STAGE 2

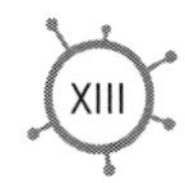

FORWARD

As an industry manager, executive recruiter, recruiting and sales trainer, event speaker, and as VP of a nationwide system of recruitment offices, I have seen most every aspect of the hiring process from both the internal and external view as the decision-maker, the decision-influencer, and as the objective observer. This varied insight is what provides the clarity you will find in this book.

The single most interesting moment for me in any process for which I'm involved in as an advisor, is that moment when you see first-hand what an impact you can have helping some of the very best individuals in their fields, be even better, and achieve even more.

Here's a little known secret: there are no real secrets in this book. The techniques and approaches that I will teach you, and that you will learn, have always been used by the best-of-the-best individuals in their job search activities. Where did they learn these 'secrets'? Some may be common sense, but most of these techniques, which the very best individuals use, have been garnered from their interactions and coachings by some of the finest executive recruiters with which they may have worked over their years of career progression.

My goal for this book is to share those insights and little known secrets with you, so that you can more effectively compete and get that next challenge, whether that is for your next career step or for your dream job.

The challenges put forth here are both real and realistic. They may certainly stretch the boundaries of comfort, but when embraced and embodied, they will help you achieve what once seemed unattainable.

I would love to hear from you as you take on, and challenge yourself, and so would others, so visit my website at www.SelfRecruiter.com and share your experiences.

John Crant

INTRODUCTION

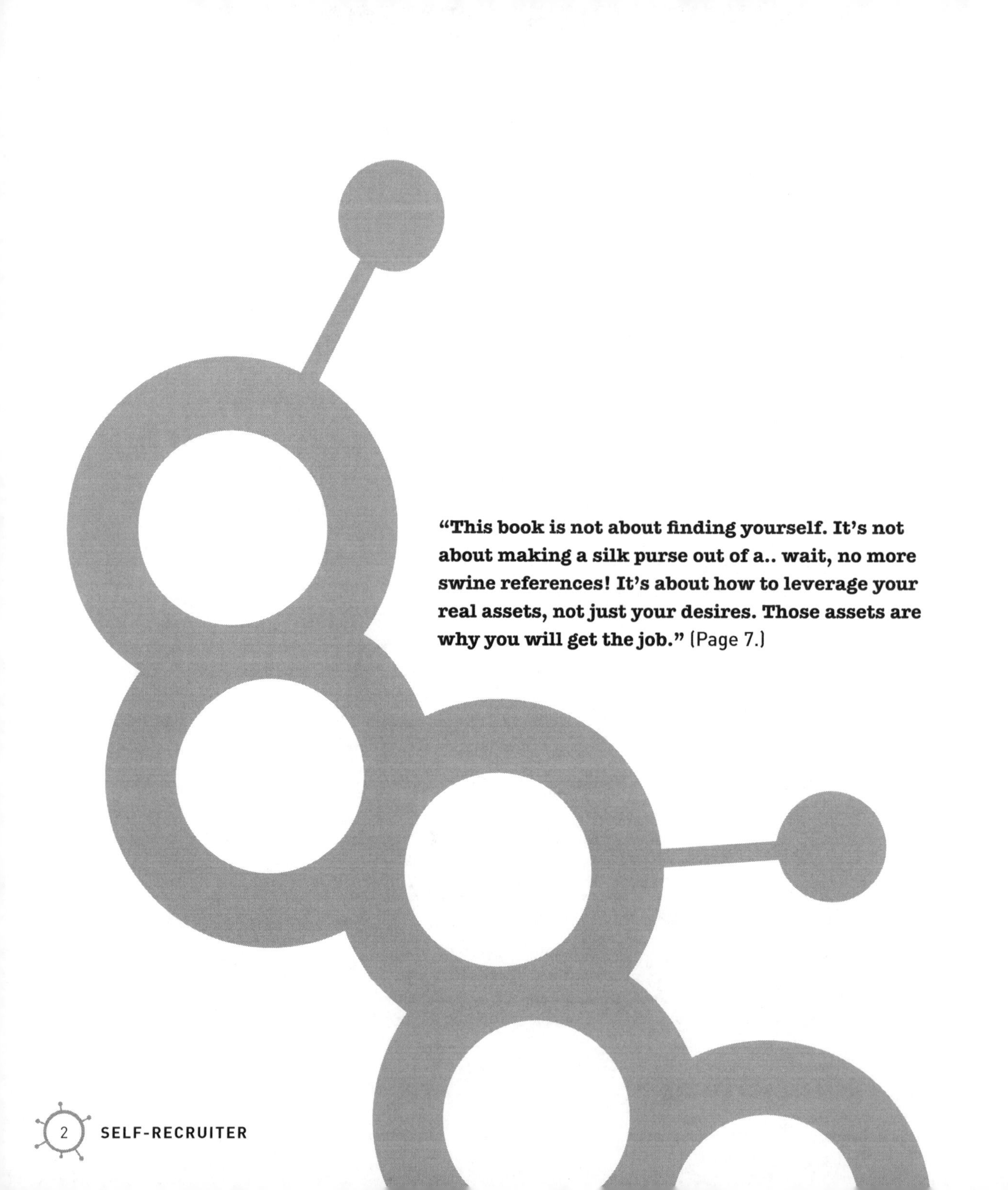

"This book is not about finding yourself. It's not about making a silk purse out of a.. wait, no more swine references! It's about how to leverage your real assets, not just your desires. Those assets are why you will get the job." (Page 7.)

INTRODUCTION

WELCOME

Congratulations (for the work you are about to do)

Really. Congratulations- you just took on a serious challenge, one that you may not be sure you are up to meeting. That, a period of challenging oneself in an unfamiliar area, is where magic can happen.

I still believe in making magic happen. Maybe not the tricks you performed as a child at family gatherings, but taking on, and making, the unexpected or unattainable happen. Simply being willing to take on the challenges that I will put forward to you in this book will make you a better candidate for your next position, significantly increase your chances for success in each role you apply for in your job search, and make you a better employee that contributes more to your company. Now that is someone a hiring manager wants to hire, especially when companies face many of the same types of challenges that you may be experiencing personally.

Why, Why Now and How this Book will help you as a Personal Specialist and Coach.

Over the last ten years, I have worked as a recruiter in several fields and industries, and they all have a central commonality: people, human and social nature, combined with different styles and methods companies use in their hiring process. It can feel scary and out of control.

"Why haven't they called me? I'm perfect."
"Why did I not get that second or third interview, or an offer?"
"Why did they offer me so much less than I was expecting?"
"Why do I feel like they think I'm not qualified?"

And endless others.

Doubt and insecurity creep in and, little by little, you grow less and less confident. You may seem to be a weaker candidate as more time goes on without finding that right next step in your work-life. It can become a self fulfilling prophecy of missed opportunities.

Change the Cycle, and Change the Rules.

I never met a rule I didn't like (to break).

We all know them: the rules. Social and work convention has slowly stripped the humanity from the hiring process. We apply. We wait and wait. We call, but rarely get any meaningful answers. Sometimes they never call. But what happened? (Answer: You followed the 'Rules')

Hiring managers and HR professionals are too busy and overworked, just like everyone else these days. They have real work to do and participating and driving their own hiring process is just one small part of their responsibilities and challenges that have to be met. More and more on their plates, until vital things (like great candidates) begin to fall off the pile. Lost opportunity for the candidates, the hiring managers, HR, and the company's stockholders, who will ultimately feel the results when the best talent slips away and the aggregate results of this happening again and again result in the company's lower shareholder earnings.

This key reality of the modern business world is why the recruiting business can exist. Companies and hiring managers need an expert, a specialist that will not take their eye off the ball and, in the end, will provide them with individuals that are not just 'capable' of doing the job, but exceptional. And exceptional individuals add to a company's bottom line, regardless of their role.

So, why not just find a recruiter that specializes in your niche? You could, and maybe should, but in this market and economic climate, recruiters are facing many of the same challenges and frustrations, along with lack of results that individuals are facing. Everyone is closing the purse strings trying to cut costs (of course, now is just the time that companies should be using really great recruiters even more). In my experience over the last ten years as a recruiter, recruiting and sales trainer, and as VP of a nationwide system of recruitment offices, the numbers never lie. The reality is that even in a good market, for every candidate a good recruiter interviews and qualifies as a 'good candidate for their niche', ultimately that recruiter will only place 1 to 2 out of every 100. Scary, I know. It's a sales business and sales is always about getting past many, many of the typical responses and rejections, until you finally get that yes. Recruiters may seem to be paid quite handsomely by their client companies, but they work extremely hard for each result that comes to fruition. Typically, only the very best of the best candidates in any niche will find occasional success through a recruiter (from a candidate's perspective). The companies know and understand the value that recruiters offer and that's why they are (usually) willing to pay recruiters for help.

But in these times, you really need to be your own specialist, your own career counselor, and your own recruiter: a Self-Recruiter.

And I'll teach you how. I'll demystify the process step by step, and without the 'filter'. I'll show you how to begin to take back the control and how to 'drive' your own hiring process with companies for which you want to work. And along the way, I'll share the secrets and insights recruiters use to benefit their clients and candidates.

You'll learn how to get your resume noticed and get that next interview. How to reach out directly to hiring managers and how to beat the other candidates that you are competing against. You'll learn how to build chemistry with anyone you meet. You'll learn how to negotiate a better offer with a better salary. I'll teach you how to avoid common traps in the Human Resources department. How to utilize the Internet resources available to you. How to plan for the unexpected and I'll teach you how to plan, set goals, and manager your job search.

Taking that first step back toward control can be a very difficult one whether your confidence may be suffering after a layoff, restructuring or even while you are still employed but worrying about your future security with your current company.

The techniques that I will teach you here are the necessary steps for you to learn, grow and get that right next career challenge. You will grow in ways that will add to your performance successes, both immediately and long into your future.

This book is not about finding yourself. It's not about making a silk purse out of a.. wait, no more swine references! It's about how to leverage your real assets, not just your desires. Those assets are why you will get the job.

So, what are you waiting for?

Let's Get Going!

I'm A Product!? Answer: Yes!

What's your favorite product, the one that you rave to others about? Your iPhone, iPod, Wii, TIVO or the latest 52" TV maybe? Or maybe it's that little cafe's homemade pie that you enjoy. No matter, really, the question is about understanding what a hot product is, and how your desire for it feels.

You are a product too.
Companies and hiring managers 'buy' you (or at least your time and talents) when they make you an offer which you accept and hire you for their team. So if there's a buyer, that means there's a seller too, and it's you. How uncomfortable does that sound? The discomfort with the buy/sell portion of the hiring process is also why candidates often accept less than they should, be it about money or potential responsibilities in the role.

> **Understanding 'desire' one feels for a hot product will help you understand that companies can feel that desire for a sharp, top-notch candidate as well.**

Let's check-in on reality and see how we can create that desire for the next hot hiring product (that would be you!).

Reality Check: Self

You are committed to being the best candidate that you can be, right?

Okay... your first assignment:

Get naked in front of a mirror, with only florescent-lighting.

Instantly the fear wells up. Nothing can be more jarring to our ego than facing an assault of imperfections and a reality that we cannot escape. Without our clothes to hide behind, we are forced to face the truth: most of us don't, and will never, look like all those people on TV and in the magazines. The florescent light is like a polygraph of our physical state of being. And you cannot escape the truth. But, it can be a good motivator to get us to the gym.

Let's do the same thing for our work assets:

> **Where am I staring from?**
> **(the only way to understand how to navigate and reach your goal)**

We need to shine the light of our 'naked, florescent-lighting' test on our resume, our job history, our achievements and credits, and on our 'Work Pedigree' (how companies and hiring managers look at our current and past employers to gage our value in the marketplace). Only by coming face to face with reality and acknowledging it, can we then correct or improve each area resulting in a better product, and a better you.

GET OVER IT!

Taking that first step back toward control can be a very difficult one whether your confidence may be suffering after a layoff, restructuring or even while you are still employed, but worrying about your future security with your current company.

Many great, productive and talented employees get laid off too. There's the perception in our minds that once laid off, others may see us as the 'bottom 10%' (Thanks to Jack & GE). While continually cutting or replacing the bottom 10% may have real merits for a business' performance (not to mention being a really great motivator for others in the company to work very, very hard), if we end up laid off, it can be a difficult blow to our ego and confidence.

Get over it. Period. Of course, do a realistic self-assessment and correct and improve any areas that may need it, but great people do get laid off too, so put the guilt up an a shelf and out of your way.

Reality Check: Others' Eyes

Understanding how others may estimate your value, and how to win them over to your perspective, will serve you well as a Self-Recruiter.

Many people put little effort into improving (not fabricating) their resume, or their other tangibles and intangibles which they have to offer. They may have a decent work history with well-known companies and feel that managers will just 'pick them'.

> **What they forget is that if you are being considered for a position, the manager is also considering at least 6 to 8 other top contenders (or possibly many more these days).**

It's not simply about you and your assets, it's about how you compare, and what you can bring to the company or to the manager's team, compared with all the others that are competing against you for the position. So, you are competing against other products that you can not even see or evaluate. But you do have an imagination, so imagine the 'best of the best', and how you will position and sell your skills to the manager so that you are the right, next hot product they will choose.

THE (SECRET) TRUTH ABOUT RECRUITERS

The Good, The Bad, and The Ugly
A word about Recruiters.

Some of my best friends are recruiters.
There are many very fine and sharp recruiters for every niche.

Unfortunately, there are also many, many that are not so sharp, and they fall into the category of being basic telemarketers. If you are also working with a recruiter while you are pursuing opportunities on your own, do your best to be sure that they are one of the better ones at what they do.

Good or bad market aside: It's a numbers game:

> The reality is, that even in a good market, for every candidate that a good recruiter interviews and qualifies as a 'good, qualified candidate for their niche', ultimately that recruiter will only place 1 to 2 out of every 100.

Scary, I know.

Now factor in a business environment where companies themselves are struggling to survive.

Think of jobs in a company being organized into a pyramid, foundational jobs are at the bottom, with various layers of professional and management positions in the middle. The top positions and top managers in each discipline are at the, well, top.

That's a fairly traditional pyramid with the base forming a wide foundation to support the less-and-less number of higher-level positions that are above. But, in these times of such economic upheaval, the pressure is on the entire structure and causing it to falter. When the business world seems to be turned onto its ear, or even worse, what is happening to the pyramid? Visual:

> The top of the Pyramid
> (because it's upside down and at risk of collapse)
> can't sustain it's finances and something has to give.

Just like an individual or family experiencing severe financial issues, companies are scrambling as their sources of capital and lines of credit (which they use to pay the operational costs of their businesses) are drying up. Payroll and other expenses cannot be met and something has to be cut, and quickly. The upside-down pyramid has to rapidly shed blocks at the 'base' before the whole structure gives way. Many companies have already shed the necessary weight to increase their likelihood of survival, but they are still working day and night to shed more and more expenses (hint: less and less new jobs available, and less and less recruiters being able to work/get paid by companies until the companies have recovered).

Now, more than ever, you need to take control and be your own recruiter:
a Self-Recruiter focused on just one great candidate -YOU.

GETTING STARTED

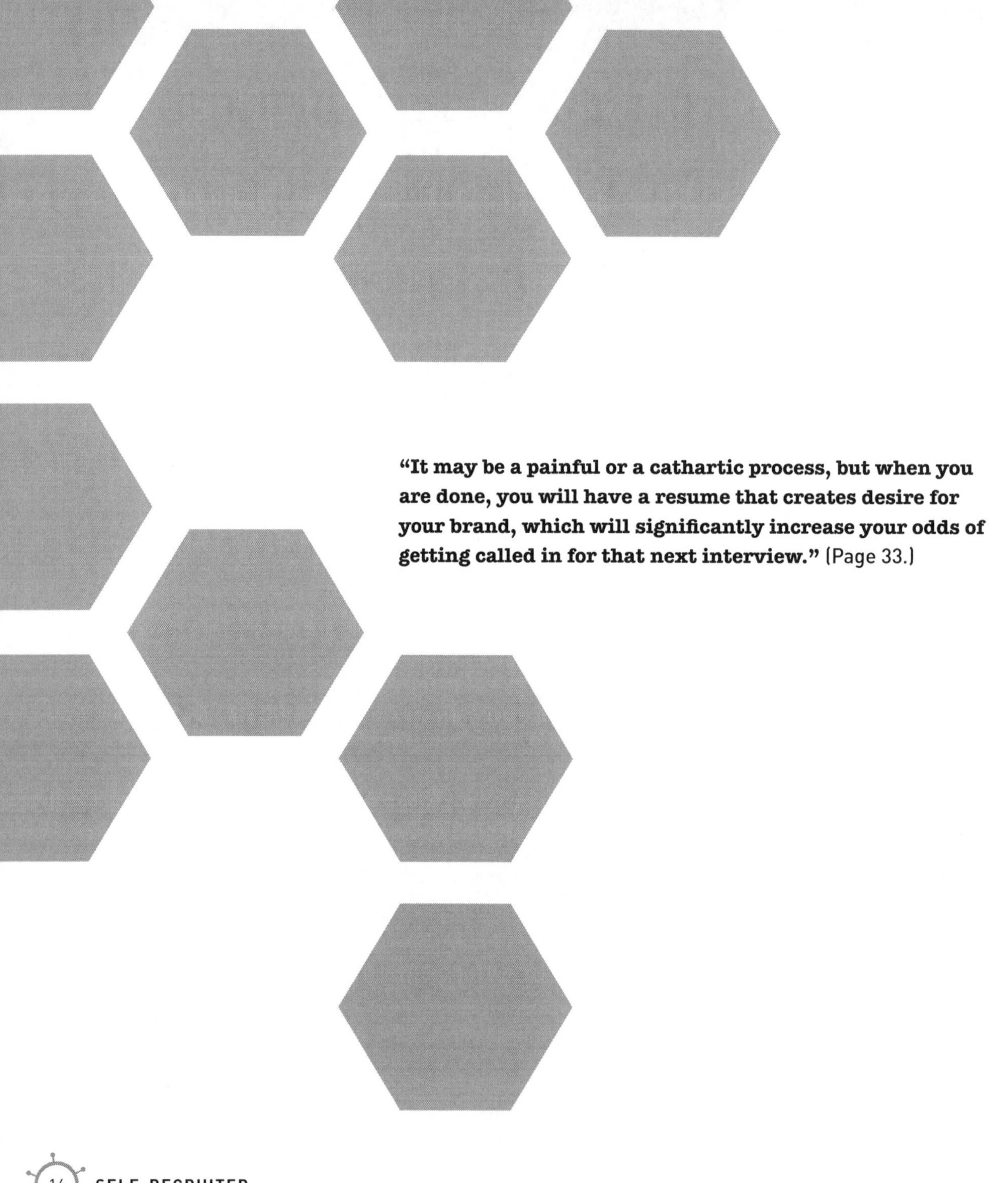

"It may be a painful or a cathartic process, but when you are done, you will have a resume that creates desire for your brand, which will significantly increase your odds of getting called in for that next interview." (Page 33.)

GETTING STARTED

No Matter Your Industry, Position or Level, It's About Sales

It may seem strange to begin our journey by talking about sales, but if you are to become a Self-Recruiter, you will need to understand some basics, even if your usual role has nothing to do with sales.

> **No matter the role you may specialize in during your career, when you are looking for a new career challenge, it's about selling a product: You.**

Applying for a position, interviewing over the telephone or in-person, writing a cover letter, preparing and presenting your resume are all activities that you may be familiar with from changing jobs during your work-life. Because most of us do not change jobs all the time or interview for a living, we really have far less experience at it than we believe. Had 2, 5 or even 10 jobs during your career? When you add up the time you may have invested preparing yourself, and going through various hiring processes, it's really very little time - when compared to your genuine area of expertise (being great at your role for a company and your position while employed). Not to mention that many times, there are at least a few years between these life-changing events. Use it or loose it, as the saying goes.

It's difficult to be an expert at selling yourself when you only do it a few times every number of years.

Even folks that are sales professionals, and sell all the time in their role, may think they 'sell themselves' while selling their company's products or services, and they are right -to a small degree. But there's a vast difference in understanding how to position and sell your abilities, expertise and leveraging your assets to get that right next career move and simply selling your company's product to a customer.

Using some of the best techniques of recruiters, you can learn to effectively sell yourself to a potential employer. So, let's put on our 'Sales' hat.

But I Hate Salespeople!

The first question that I like to ask my audience when teaching a seminar is, "What do you think of Sales People?

Many times, after an awkward moment of silence, someone blurts out, "I hate salespeople!"

The poor, maligned salesperson. Well, I'm a salesperson too, but I take no offense at the statement. In reality, I know they don't mean it -even if they think that they do. What they hate are bad sales people, people that do not know how to sell well.

In a way, the question I threw to my audience was a trap, and they fell right into it. See, certain questions, and the way you construct them, cause an immediate 'image response' in your brain. I say something, and an image just 'pops' into their brain uncontrollably. Don't believe me?

Let me demonstrate:

Clear you mind and try hard to resist thinking of any image.
Really... don't let me take control of your brain function.

Okay, now we're ready for the demonstration, and here it is:

Think for a moment of the most favorite teacher you ever had...

Is that image in your head? If not, you may be wired the other direction and I simply have to reverse the question:

Think for a moment of the teacher you hated the most.

For virtually everyone, one or both of those images will 'pop' into their consciousness.

Learning that technique, and how to utilize it, is part of becoming an effective sales professional. And that's what you need to become to sell yourself to a potential employer.

So, why do people hate sales people?

They don't, they just 'pop' images of experiences of the 'sales processes' that they did not enjoy. Can you think of a car salesman that you 'enjoyed' working with, while buying a car in the past? Now, that's a tough one to make work sometimes!

The truth is there are (some) great car sales individuals, just like there are (some) great recruiters. But the sales question makes us respond to the process of being 'sold to', and most times we did not enjoy that process because they were not very good sales people.

In Sales, Less is More (stop at the buy sign)

Okay, so you've decided to accept my challenge of enhancing your abilities to include selling you own assets and expertise. Great! In Stage 2, I will teach you specifically what you can, and should, say about yourself and how to do it as if it was for your living - after all, your earnings and future great positions depend upon it. For now, let's just think and absorb a few basics on sales in general. In this process, you'll develop a deeper realization of your assets and how they are viewed by others, so much so, that we will need to keep in mind the major guideline for sales success:

> **Less is more, and to stop at the buy-sign.**

Less, but very specific and valuable information, is much more helpful in our efforts than the 'everything plus-the-kitchen-sink' approach.

> **You have to know what you are selling (you),**
> **who you are selling to (the hiring manager), and**
> **why they would be 'making the best business decision'**
> **that they could make, by hiring you.**

Knowing oneself, your assets, and how to position them when speaking or leaving a voice mail for a potential hiring manager can be a difficult task without clarity. Many individuals with really fine backgrounds fail to present and properly take credit for what they have to offer. Under the

'Resume Renovation' section, I'll teach you how to add clarity and see yourself as potential hiring managers do. And that will give you the ability and confidence to better sell yourself to them.

In addition to knowing your product (you), you need to understand who the buyer is - in this case, the hiring manager. There are many resources at your disposal to find out in advance about a particular hiring manager, and I'll show you how. Everything you are able to uncover will help you better connect and communicate with the manager during your 'sales process', which is better know by its usual description, as their hiring process. We'll cover this process of discovery and outreach in further detail in the 'Who Ya Gonna Call?' section.

Lastly, to better sell yourself, you need to understand why it would be in their best interests to hire you.

Only then can you understand how to persuade the manager that you are the best choice for their needs.

In the following sections, I'll help you better prepare and package that new product, you, for 'selling' during the hiring process. And we'll develop what to say about your experience and expertise, along with understanding how to take control back in the hiring process.

Resume Renovation

The Truth, The Whole Truth, and Nothing But The Truth... Just with a better spotlight with which to shine

Dust off that old resume and let's get started. As with any renovation, we have to be prepared and ready for it to get a little messy. Your resume is not a biography. It's not even a 'light read' covering your entire background.

A Resume:

What is it? It is, and should be, that simple 'Sales Sheet' on a hot product that you want to help create that 'desire' for, that we had talked about.

Creating that intangible desire for that 'next great thing', that we all feel sometimes when looking in a store window, will serve you well -once you develop it on your resume.

Let's tear down some walls. Ever done a renovation on part of a home that you love? Think of a bathroom or kitchen renovation. The dust, the dirt, the mess. Well, if you are like me, the first thing you do is to try to cover and protect the rest of the items in the house. After all, many of those items are personal to you and you've formed an attachment to them. You certainly don't want to lose them. It's the same when looking at, and beginning to renovate, your resume. Many items listed, and

HUNGRY YET?

Let me give you an analogy that is a great visual of our challenges and our goals with regards to your resume.

Think about the last time you went out to an expensive restaurant:

You placed your order for an appetizer, entree, vegetable, etc. Question: When your $12 to $15 appetizer arrived, how large was it? Usually, the more expensive the restaurant, the smaller the appetizer. How come? Well, it may be because they want more profit, but also it's because they understand its function during your meal.

One look in the dictionary will remind us all of what the appetizer's purpose is:

> "... to stimulate the appetite and create a desire for more food."

It's not to satisfy the desire for food, but rather the opposite.

In a similar way, your resume is not the 'entree' that should satisfy all the manager's hunger for knowledge about you, it is the appetizer.

> Your resume's job is to 'awaken' the desire of the potential employer to want to hear more.

Once that is achieved, any additional information has the power, and the possibility, of actually lessening your value. So, add what is valuable and necessary, and leave out, was is not. That way, they will be hungry for more and excited to interview you.

accomplishments you may have achieved, may be like the items in your house, and you may have developed a strong personal attachment to them over time -and that's okay. Just be prepared to take them out of your resume anyway.

> **Remember, it's not about creating a laundry list of simply everything, it's about creating focused value.**

Okay, so you are ready for resume cuts, but where should you start? Answer: With the goals in mind!

The goals for your resume renovation, your 'own personal sales sheet', are clear.

Resume Goal:

A clean, clear, and straightforward format. A format where the information jumps off of the page for the reader. Specific items and accomplishments are included thought to be of greatest interest to the hiring manager, formatted in such a way so they can be easily absorbed at first glance. And, a clear accounting of your educational background and any ongoing training which may be relevant.

Let's change the way we look at resumes for a minute and think about it from the hiring manager's eyes. HR individuals and hiring managers may get many resumes for a particular opening. The advertisement goes up, and resumes pour in and they begin to stack up. Well, HR professionals and hiring managers have real, other work, to do -not just doing interviews and managing their own hiring processes. Before long, each resume is getting only a few seconds of 'look-time' before they need to make a quick decision as to which stack they should be sorted into.

Those stacks are:

(1.) **'I need to look at these',**

(2) **'There might be someone in here and I may look sometime later'**, and

(3) the **'thanks-but-no-thanks'** stack, where they place those resumes that they have deemed 'not a fit' for some reason.

Here's a secret that you may not like:

As the hiring manager or HR professional gets busier and busier and works toward sorting those incoming resumes, the time allotted to making that quick assessment before dividing resumes into stacks can become very, very short. How short?

> **It can be just 3 to 5 seconds per resume.**

A friend of mine was recently pursuing an art director position with a major university's communications department. It's an attractive position with great benefits and an opportunity to run a nice-sized design studio. Within the first three hours of the job being posted, they had over 600 resumes sent in. How would it even be possible to read every resume fully at the rate they were being delivered? The answer, of course, is that it is not possible, if the manager is to accomplish any of their other work. The reality is that, the managers and HR professionals that are very good, learn to skim resumes very quickly looking for that right combination of qualities and then they sort, sort, sort.

> **Your first goal in this challenge is to get your resume, your sales sheet, into stack number one.**

My goal is to help you achieve that by showing you where and how to cut items within your resume. This will help you move toward a format that takes the work away for the reader, simply letting the information, and your value, just flow uninhibited right into their brains.

One Page Resume, Unless It's Two :-(

Understanding how to read a resume in 3 to 5 seconds will help you make the cuts that you need to on your own sales sheet.

In order to accomplish our goal, our resume and value needs to be able to be absorbed at first glance. What are the key elements that we want them to know instantly?

(1.) Our Name, which is our brand.
(2.) The current/last 3 employers and titles of the positions that we held.
(3.) Our educational background.

Try this:

Count out loud, **"One thousand-one, one thousand-two, one thousand-three."**

You now have a fresh 'feel' for how short 3 seconds really is, and an understanding of the effective time limit we are working within.

Okay, now pick up your resume:

In the same time length we just verbalized, see how easily you can accomplish 'absorbing' your 3 key points, as outlined above.

Your resume should be one single page, in most every case. Yes, there are cases where you might be wise to use a two page format, but never longer than that. Just keep visualizing stacks and stacks of resumes and you can quickly understand why a single-page, well-formatted resume full of sharp accomplishments gets noticed quickly.

Let's breakdown your resume by sections.

I Object! To Objectives, most of the time.

Objectives and personal summaries can be important for some cases, such as an individual new to the workforce or when planning a change of industries, but for many, they take up all-to-valuable resume space with repeated information. While repetition has its place, especially in the teaching of new ideas, it is of little use on a resume.

> **Remember, don't lose site of the goal:**
> **a simple sales sheet that catches attention and**
> **gets you the interview.**

We're making progress now, so let's break a few more walls.

Your Work Pedigree (Yes, Your Work History Builds Your Value)

We may now get the '3 to 5 second review' of our resume, but we may not yet understand how they are 'valuing' us, based upon that quick look. Here's an example:

Todd Smith

Employment:
Nestle USA, Inc.
Director of (QA) Quality Assurance

Kraft Foods, Inc.
Quality Assurance (QA) Manager

The Coca-Cola Company, Inc.
Quality Assurance Engineer

Education:
University of Florida
BS in Agriculture

With just a quick glance, and the proper formatting (which I'll show you in the next section), an HR professional or hiring manager looks at the

(1.) quality of the companies for which you have worked,
(2.) the titles that you have held, and
(3.) your educational background

- and from that, they make a quick judgement about 'your value', as compared to other resumes they will review.

How do you think this manager might compare 'Todd's value', as shown in the example, to another resume showing the same experience with three employers that he had not heard of before? While you cannot change past employers that you have chosen to work for, you can build your value going forward when choosing your next employer, keeping in mind that you also have a brand to build: your own.

Value, Value, Everywhere. But Nowhere to be Seen.

If there is a single area where candidates lose more value on their resumes, it's in what they write under each Employer/Title. For an employer that may not be well-known, you should consider including a statement reflecting

(1.) who they are, that also reflects
(2.) why your experience working for them may be of value to your next employer.

That may not be necessary with many well-known companies, particularly if you specialize within a niche that is well defined, with a number of companies that are aware of one another.

Achievements listed under the Employer/Title should be bullet-pointed for easiest absorption, and be written with very specific tangibles or deliverables. Always look for

(1.) where you saved the company money, or
(2.) where you increased revenues, or
(3.) where you increased efficiency or decreased inefficiency or affected performance in some way.

Just listing your duties is not very valuable. How you affected the company's bottom line, by some of your actions, will always get you noticed and increase 'your value' too, as they will look for similar results, should they choose to hire you.

Be sure to cite specific items you have accomplished, like:

- **Reduced QA rejection rate** by **34%** within the first six months in the role.
- **Increased Sales for territory** by **26%** to $**1.5M**.
- **Achieved $30K** in **Cost Reductions** by reorganizing / consolidating 2 departments.

Achievements without the specifics ($, %, etc.) read like no achievements (no value) at all.

Degrees of Degrees

Let's look at your educational achievements. Your educational profile can help or hurt you, depending on how it is handled. Many great and highly productive employees also may not have a completed college degree. This may be a very important factor in the hiring process for some positions, and of less importance in others.

What is important: The Truth.

The truth, the whole truth, and nothing but the truth. Now, while even attending a college or university is an achievement, let's not parse words.

Do you have, or have you received in hand, your college degree?

This question may seem strange to some, but in my ten years in the recruiting industry, I've had to ask that question over and over again, because of unclear handling on a resume. Like my earlier sidebar, 'Get Over It', if you did not receive your degree (and there is really is no in-between on this), that's fine, but get over it. I'm not making judgements. You may have gained even more valuable industry expertise that is also sellable to a hiring manager, than just what the degree would have given you. But, you must be honest, and, you must be straightforward.

If you are 3 credits shy of your degree, to list a Bachelors degree on your resume is, well, BS. This is not the area of your background which you want to become involved in a protracted discussion about, during any stage of your interview process. It just creates doubt about whether you would be the best individual for the position. Choose instead to focus on other accomplishments that you have achieved, and be very clear about your educational achievements with something such as, "Coursework toward a BS in Electrical Engineering" (if that was your educational path) placed under the name of the college or university that you had attended. Do not list the degree itself, because you will likely mislead, and that could cost you the job offer at the last minute, when they conduct background and reference checks. I have seen candidates lose an offer over this exact situation, even when the degree was not a requirement for the position. Remember, no one wants to begin a new relationship with someone that misleads from the first date. It's the same when looking for your next career home.

Be sure to include all trainings, seminars and other ongoing educational coursework that you have completed, but only if relevant and of interest to a potential hiring manager considering you for a specific role.

When in doubt, less is usually more.

First Impressions (Can be difficult to overcome!)

Are You Out of Control?

Success in life can come at unexpected times, but usually, it comes from a hard, consistent effort toward your goals. Having, and maintaining, control over how potential employers form their views about you is easier than you think (to lose control of).

Designing your resume... Isn't it just a Word Doc?

Are you a Creative Professional? Okay, you have my permission for a 'designed' or unconventional resume. As an example, an art director's or graphic designer's resume that has not been 'designed' would be a fatal flaw, since that niche is focused on visual communication design.

But, for everyone else, what I mean by 'designing your resume' is simply that you should spend more time than just dumping your text into Microsoft Word. Using Word to design your resume is fine for most, but I will tell you shortly why you should then be converting it to a PDF file format, before sending out to a potential employer.

Design starts with the right content.

Look closely at the next few pages of example resumes and notice how they, while each being from different industries, just 'flow' as you try to skim and absorb the contents. Part of that easy flow is from the necessary, if difficult, cuts that each individual has made. The rest of the achievement in 'flow', comes from formatting choices. Font size choices, use of bold and italics, underlines, as well as other accents, each have a large impact on flow and readability. As you refine your formatting, keep in mind the goals are...

> **... to move your brand forward by adding focus to you (your name) and help the reader visualize your brand value and career path, achievements, etc., as well as clearly informing them about your educational background.**

It may be a painful or a cathartic process, but when you are done, you will have a resume that creates desire for your brand, which will significantly increase your odds of getting called in for that next interview.

RESUME EXAMPLE 1

Jason Smith

325 First Avenue, Atlanta, GA 30301 770-XXX-XXXX info@providentresource.com

---

SUMMARY:

15+ Years in Logistics / Supply Chain

EXPERIENCE

Bed, Bath & Beyond, Inc., Atlanta, GA — 2004 - Present
Director of Distribution

- **Senior supply chain management executive** for a **$9.5B enterprise**.
- **Create strategies** for optimization of supply chain processes and technologies.
- **Identify synergies and facilitate consolidation** of disciplines/processes/personnel between many individual, disparate divisions.
- Responsible for corporate transportation contracts / expenditures **exceeding $80M**.

Bed, Bath & Beyond, Inc., Atlanta, GA — 2000 - 2004
Director of Transportation

- **Responsible for distribution center** (DC) operations /freight consolidation for **$2.5B in sales.**
- **2,500 SKUs** through a **network of 24 third-party** dry/conditioned DCs.
- **$38M operating budget** for DCs; **$50M operating budget** for freight-consolidation.

buy buy Baby, Inc., Atlanta, GA — 1998 - 2000
Director of Logistics

- Supply chain management executive for a **$1.7B food processing company**.
- Responsible for **$98M annual spend** and **managing 500 associates**. Customer Service, Transportation, Fleet Maintenance and Warehouse functions.
- **Responsible for transforming supply chain processes, systems and facilities** to create the premier supply chain in the poultry industry.
- **Led internal team** to identify opportunities, articulate and gain board approval, and implement strategies.

SYSCO Corporation, Atlanta, GA — 1994 - 1998
Manager of Logistics

Target, Inc., Atlanta, GA — 1992 - 1994
Finance & Asset Manager, Logistics Division

Target, Inc., Atlanta, GA — 1990 - 1992
Sr. Internal Auditor

EDUCATION

University of Georgia, Athens, GA
BS, in Marketing — 1988 - 1992

RESUME EXAMPLE 2

Jill Stevens

309 West 29th Street, Apt. 20R, New York, NY 10001 917.XXX.XXXX info@providentresource.com

EXPERIENCE

Limited Brands / Victoria's Secret, New York, NY 2007 - Present
Regional Manager

- **Senior District Manager Northeast/ NY Metro.**
- **#1 Region, 2008** in the company.

Old Navy, Inc., New York, NY 2000 - 2007
Regional Director

- **Directing a 77 store region** generating **annual sales of $450M**
- **Developed 11 key Managers** [3 District Managers; 2 to Regional Directors; 1 Sr. Manager Store Profit Optimization; & 5 District Managers.
- **Decreased Shortage 25%.**
- **#1 Region, 2005** in the company.
- **Recognized by Senior Vice President** 2004 District Manager s Conference

Urban Outfitters, Inc., New York, NY 1998 - 1999
District Manager

Club Monaco, Inc., New York, NY 1997 - 1998
General Manager

Gap, Inc., New York, NY 1995 - 1997
District Manager

- **Managed 21 stores in 2 states**, generating **annual sales of $49M**
- **Received Words to Live By Award** for Everyone Counts in 1997
- **Nominated for President's Award** in 1996
- **Recognized for highest Profit Contribution** results 1996
- **Recognized for Operational Excellence** results 1995

Gap, Inc., New York, NY 1993 - 1995
Store Manager

- **Managed $17 M Flagship,** location based in Manhattan
- **Responsible for all aspects of P & L** including store compliance audits, security services, store scheduling and merchandise processing/ replenishment.
- **Invited to the Regional Manager Conference**, 1995

EDUCATION

Fashion Institute of Technology, New York, NY 1990 - 1994
BS in Retail Merchandising

RESUME EXAMPLE 3

Ed Lornsefferd

65 Forestriver Circle., Philadelphia, PA 19019 C: 610-XXX-XXXX info@providentresource.com

SENIOR PROGRAM, ACCOUNT and OPERATIONS MANAGER

PROFESSIONAL EXPERIENCE

NOKIA / NOKIA SIEMENS NETWORKS, Philadelphia, PA 2006-Present
Global industry leader of communications services providing complete product portfolio of mobile and fixed network infrastructure solutions.
Regional Care Manager

- **Responsible for all Care** phase operations through improvement of customer satisfaction, provision of care services and development of new business.
- **Profit and Loss Responsibility** for two of the largest **AT&T / Cingular** markets: Philadelphia and Washington-Baltimore, as well as Nokia-Siemens' largest sub-regional account (Tier 2) : **Chinook Wireless** d.b.a. **Montana PCS**: Total of **$20M revenue**
- Experienced in end-to-end convergence solutions and platforms, service and device management solutions, access and transport solutions and managed services and hosting.

TRUEPOSITION, LIBERTY MEDIA, Berwyn, PA 2004-2005
World's largest and leading company dedicated exclusively to providing variety of wireless location systems, applications and services.
Program Manager

- **PM** for **$250M** initiative. Implementing FCC wireless E911 mandate.
- **Successfully executed** FCC requirements in over **75 markets** with more than 20,000 sites designed, installed, tested and accepted.
- **Built and Managed Program Management team**, creating cross-functional systems as well as numerous processes and procedures to support the execution and rollout of developing product and service for customer.

LEVEL 3 COMMUNICATIONS, (formerly Genuity and GTE/Verizon), Woburn, MA 2000 – 2003
Pioneer, innovator and leader within internet industry first as BBN and then GTE Internetworking, Genuity launched as a public company in June 2000 from the merger of GTE and Bell Atlantic to create Verizon. Level 3 purchased Genuity in February 2003.
Program and Project Management; Professional Services

- **Program Manager** for **Pepsi**. one of the company's largest Managed Services customers.
- **Selected to Lead** the delivery and selling of new service of **Enterprise VOIP**. Strategic and largest customers including **Verizon**, **Smith Barney**, **Schneider Electric**, and **Lightbridge, Inc.**
- **Program Manager** for the **PhotoChannel Networks**. Implementation included DSL connectivity and VPN security with a **1st year contract value** of **$3.3M** with revenue potential of **$24M** with **7500 sites**.
- **Manager** for the **Puerto Rico Telephone Company's** (PRTC) purchase and installation of Point-of-Presence (POP) equipment / services. **1st year contract value** est. at **$5.5M**.
- **Senior Project Manager** for **Bell Atlantic** and **Genuity** partnership providing **Commonwealth of Massachusetts** internet access and VPN connectivity.

Prior Employment:

CABLE AND WIRELESS, New York, NY 1999 - 2000
KINKO'S CORPORATION, New York, NY 1993-1999
LERCH, BATES AND ASSOCIATES, New York, NY 1991-1993
OTIS ELEVATOR (subsidiary of **United Technologies**) 1984-1991

EDUCATION

Lehigh University, Bethlehem, PA.
B.A., Economics and English, double major

Professional Development:
Numerous project management (Master's Certification, George Washington University), quality, customer relations, leadership and sales programs.

LinkedIn is one of your Sales Brochures, so is Monster, Career Builder, HotJobs, among many others.

So now that you've been warned (Sidebar), how should you use these sites? Carefully. Let's divide this discussion into social-networking sites, such as LinkedIn, and the Job-Seeker websites, such as HotJobs, Career Builder, Monster and others.

Welcome to The Social

Over the last number of years, LinkedIn has become the defacto social-networking site for your work-life. There are others, but it seems to enjoy a success well beyond its competitors. Many great candidates that I uncover, are discovered through my networking activity on this site. You also need to view this site as a tremendous resource of yours, once you learn more about it, how to better utilize it, and add it to the bag containing your other Self-Recruiter tools.

In it's simplest form, the site seems to act in a similar way to functions on HotJobs, Career Builder and Monster. But there are big differences. You post/build your resume section by section and employer by employer until most or all of your resume appears

LINKEDIN, MYSPACE, FACEBOOK, TWITTER AND BEYOND. OR HAVE YOU CREATED A MONSTER?

Ever run into someone new and interesting at a party, until it turned out that they 'knew' a little too much about you from an ex? When your work-life gets judged, sometimes your non-work-life gets mixed in there too.

In the age of the Internet, we all live in a small town again. Growing up, I used to spend my summers in a very small town in Wisconsin that catered to a million-plus vacationers from across the midwest each season. My folks had a summer souvenir business where I spent each of my summers working like crazy, but I was having so much fun as well. It really was a blast. But, this was a really small town, the 'everyone-knew-everything-about-everybody' kind of town. As in any small town that has one sector that is thriving, there are always some that have more, some that have less, and those that judge everybody. Don't get me wrong, I love the town, and love the people, but I was always treated as an 'outsider'. Granted, I did not live there in the winter, since we lived in Phoenix as our year-round residence, but I was there every summer since I was in kindergarden. It didn't help that I was extremely shy (when not working with customers in our store), and that was also a difficult barrier for me to overcome. Lots of locals knew who I was, or at least who they thought I was, which, as you can guess, was not entirely accurate.

> No matter really, once that image of you is set in one's mind, it's a very difficult thing to change.

Welcome to the future and the past, forever. LinkedIn, Facebook, MySpace, Twitter and so forth may all have their place, but more and more potential employers also use those sites, so be cautious before drilling holes in the boat you are using to cross the river. The same must be considered when choosing to use HotJobs, Career Builder, or Monster, etc.

online. The similarities really end there. While the Job-Seeker sites have you post your resume to be viewed by those that pay for that access, on LinkedIn, it is not overly hidden, though you do have privacy controls in the preferences. People post to Monster or others to advertise themselves for potential jobs or employers. Only those Candidate-Seekers (that pay for access) get to see your resume. And it's a business model that has worked well and probably has its place. But LinkedIn is much more like Facebook. Each employer you add creates a link (past and present) to that company. Each school you add from your educational background creates a link to that school. Each social group you join (groups whose members have similar work specialties, as yourself) creates a link as well.

> **What LinkedIn has developed into is an open (mostly) rolodex with most profiles including a full resume, where the guilt by association also has been removed.**

Many times, if you post your resume to a Job-Seeker site, Monster in our example, others that see you there will assume you are 'on the market' and that may have real implications if your current employer happens to be the one spotting you. But with LinkedIn, it's specifically not a Job-Seeker site, so that implication has been safely and forever removed, freeing everyone to be advertising their value. Believe me, your industry or niche will likely notice if you have a sharp, valuable background posted. Since it's set up as a social-networking site, the built-in expectation is that you will also choose to link with others from your industry that may email requests-for-linking to you. As a benefit of linking, you get to search a greatly expanded pool of folks from right within your niche. You see or have the ability to search 3 levels of linked contacts - it's like seeing friends, friends-of-friends, and friends-of friends-of-friends on Facebook. It also gives you various abilities to reach out to this exponentially growing pool of people within your industry. That can be very valuable to you when considering making a change in employers.

Use this site wisely by posting and updating your background based on your new, value-filled resume. Then start linking and building your own network, for the next time you are looking to make a change.

Job-Seekers Beware

Monster, Career Builder and HotJobs, among others, have their place too, just be cautious when using them. These sites, unlike LinkedIn, usually store a 'print-ready' version of your resume. Anyone that pays for access can usually download your resume. Sounds fine, unless you consider that some less-than-scrupulous recruiters (hey- every industry has a few) can download and send your resume places without ever having spoken to you first. That is much less than ideal, to say the least. And, like I had mentioned earlier, there is even the potential that your current employer could see that you are looking. So, be careful wishing to get noticed this way.

The Gorilla, the Giraffe, the Zebra and the Snow Leopard.

Companies' 'Applicant Tracking Systems' can make you feel less than human, or at least like a zoo animal being overlooked.

Even a great zoo, like New York City's Bronx Zoo, has it's stars. If you want to know where the crowds form on a trip to the zoo, just look to its stars. Most every zoo has some. The newer, or larger or flashier animals seem to draw most of the wattage, creating a dim spotlight for others. The poor warthog and other less attractive animals seem to accept that they have been relegated to the third or forth string part of the show. Fine for the warthog, but not so fine if you are the candidate looking to find your next career challenge.

Over the past decade, more and more companies are utilizing specialize software to help them accept, track and analyze resumes that come in when potential candidates apply for positions.

> **On the surface, it doesn't sound so bad, but these databases are like an ever growing Job-Seeker website of mostly irrelevant information.**

In many cases, they result in your resume and application not receiving the best attention. All the focus and spotlight is on the daily, hourly and minute-by-minute new, flashier arrivals, with more and more of the others getting relegated to the dark and lonely recesses of the data warehouse, where your information is likely to be missed.

You've probably experienced some of these applicant systems by now. They tend to ask you inane questions that are empty and lifeless as part of your 'submission' process. More on not submitting to the inhumanity of some company's hiring processes, in the next section of the book (Stage 2/ You Can Apply, But Don't Submit!). For now, understand that participating in these company 'systems' may be a necessary evil, but they should be only one, very small, part of your efforts.

The Headless Horseman is a Great Read, But Not So, If That's How Your Resume Prints

A quick search of a major electronic office equipment website returned over 1,000 results for various printers. How will your resume look, and will it be impressive, when printing from all or most of them? Well, that can only be answered when factoring in any one of the millions of computers that might be the one used to send it to the printer. That perspective of the issue is important, and why you should not be sending a Word document as your resume. Like I had said earlier, Word is fine for most to use when formatting your resume, but if you send your resume in that same Word format, you then lose all control over its look and feel on the other end when displayed or printed. I've seen many a resume that was cut off here or there and with the text out of control. Didn't the candidate look at, and print, their resume before they sent it in for review? Of course they did! I'm not going to get into whether this is Redmond's issue or fault, but it does point out limitations that many candidates don't realize exist. The problem is with how preferences are handled within the software program, so feel free to use the program, just don't send your resume in a Word format.

The solution is a simple one, created by another software company for the Internet age. Enter, Adobe Acrobat PDF.

PDF:

which stands for Portable Document Format, is just that. It's a format where almost any document, generated by almost any piece of software, from almost any operating system, can look and print just as great, whether sent down the street or across the globe.

It works for virtually every printer used by today's businesses. You can buy your own copy of the software or you can convert a limited number of documents right on Adobe's website.

So, once you have completed your formatting magic with your Resume Renovation, don't send a resume that might end up headless ever again.

BUT, THEY ASKED FOR A WORD DOCUMENT IN THEIR JOB AD.

I ask for crazy things all the time, but rarely get them. As a recruiter, it's not unusual for me to ask candidates to go and do homework for the both of us. I ask them to come up with a list of companies that would be interested in their skill-sets. I ask them for a list of companies for which they would like to work. I ask if they could work for 'anyone' at all (no matter how crazy), who-is-it that they would like to work for most? I ask them to remember to call me immediately after they complete the interview that I had set up for them with a potential employer. If you never ask, you will 'never get', so it's not about what was requested, as I hope, you are the one that stays in control.

> Simply because they asked for a Word document in their ad is not enough of a reason to send one.

Stay in control and looking great, and send the PDF. The likely reason they may request the Word version is that the Word format may be easiest for their applicant tracking system (even just its title makes me feel like a caged animal) to understand.

If they truly need a Word version, they'll call you, and at least you'll be talking!

STAGE 2

"Don't be, it's not as difficult as it seems, and the benefits to you will help you bypass that ever-expanding waiting line in the hiring process, faster than that 'speed-pass line' for Walt Disney World's most popular rides." (Page 50)

STAGE 2

The Elevator, The Cocktail Party and the Chance Encounter (It's not what you think!)

It's about Being Ready to Get Lucky

A close friend of mine just seems to get all the things in his work-life so easily (at least to others). He moves from high-quality employer to high-quality employer with ease and has an amazing career path. He started with a long stint as a graphic designer for a well-known art school, then joined the top firm in New York within pharmaceutical advertising, as an art director. Next he moved on to a high-profile design magazine's promotions and marketing department, and then to a major New York City public institution, where he expanded his repertoire to include high-profile exhibition design. People that know him, and have watched his career progression, are amazed that he seems to just move with so little effort from one great opportunity to another. How does he do it? He's always ready to get lucky!

Those observers that think it must just be 'in the stars' for my friend, do not see all the work he does to 'get so lucky'. They do not see the efforts he makes to have the proper marketing and promotions material for himself prepared and waiting in advance for when he becomes aware of that potential great next career step. They do not see the continual networking and building of relationships within his industry that will serve him well when needed. They do not see his control and management of his own hiring process, when he is pursuing his next dream job. They do not see the confidence that all of his behind-the-scenes preparation work has given him - an amazing advantage when competing with others for that choice spot. They just see him as lucky.

> **You can get 'lucky' too, but only if you are willing to do the work necessary to make it seem so.**

The Best 25 Seconds of Your Life

Getting lucky is about being prepared. Imagine for a moment that you are lucky enough to have a chance encounter, be it in the elevator, at a cocktail party or where ever that may be, with an individual that is a key mover-and-shaker in your industry or niche. What would you say to them? Would you just gush and faun all over them as an admirer, hoping that they might remember you someday? Or might you use that opportunity to speak to them as an equally interesting individual, if still an up and comer? With little preparation, I doubt most of us would be happy with what we were able to achieve by the time those elevator doors opened and our moment of fortune had passed.

Twenty-five seconds is just long enough to satisfy.
It's the right amount of time for us to capsulize and answer two major points about ourselves and communicate those to the individual that we may meet during any such chance encounter:

(1.) Who we are, and,
(2.) Why we are interesting or memorable.

Just as your resume has experienced a spike in its value as a marketing tool from working through the necessary cuts and additions, so too will your capsulation and refinement of the best 25 seconds about you.

My recommendations here will be broad, since my readers will be from the full spectrum of industries and disciplines. You will need a specialist to help you understand the best way to communicate your very specific and best points.

Self, let me introduce you to... yourself.

> **You can be your own best specialist, as part of being a Self-Recruiter, if you can be honest with just one person: You.**

It requires quite a bit of that florescent light we had spoken about, but you can shine that light on your value. Look to what you are most passionate about when cataloguing your achievements and focus in on those.

Exercise:

In order to get started, ask yourself:

"What am I most proud of accomplishing...
in my current job?
past job(s)?

"Is there something unique or exceptional about my educational background?"

"Is there some other unique or special reason I may be an exceptional in my field?"

"If a manager was interviewing two other individuals that are the best-of-the-best, why would they hire me, over the other two?"

There can be many other selling points and questions you could ask, but the point of this exercise is to develop one or two very interesting and unique things about yourself and then you have the basics to incorporate in your small talk when this chance encounter happens to you.

Learn to Love Role-Playing.
Find a friend that can be objective and who is willing to role-play with you. If you do not practice what you might say at one of these chance encounters, you will not likely be ready when your opportunity arrives.

Exercise:

Assume that you and your 'industry mover-and-shaker' are in the elevator alone, and the doors have just closed.

Now, as scary and embarrassing as it seems, verbally reach out to them and find an effective way to combine your greeting and acknowledgement of them along with why you admire their achievements, with a segue to your self-introduction which includes your Best 25 Seconds.

And don't forget to give them your business card - and get theirs. This will be very helpful and useful to you in dropping them a note to reinforce the positives of your chance meeting. Not to mention it will be much easier now to reach out and link with them professionally, on LinkedIn.

You Want Me to Be a Telemarketer? NO!

Everything in this world has it's place, even telemarketers (just don't be one for this project!).

Last night we made a delicious meal. It was a spanish paella, cooked to perfection, with chicken, sausage, shrimp and muscles and even a half lobster on top. My mouth just melted as I scooped the contents from the pot and arranged the feast on each plate. Steaming hot and spectacular. It's one of my favorite special dinners that we make on occasion and last night my fork was so anxious to offer up that first taste of perfection. But, then my phone rang and it was... the dreaded telemarketer. Now everything has its time and place in this world (and I think I know where the telemarketer's place should be), but just as I'm about to experience culinary nirvana is neither the time nor the place, in my humble opinion.

Our reaction to the telemarketer is understandable, as it has triggered our memory of dislike for the sales process (if not that for sales people).

> **So I'm going to ask you to attempt the very difficult as your next challenge on the road to becoming a Self-Recuiter:**
>
> **Calling hiring individuals to introduce yourself,
> just like you did with the chance encounter in the elevator.**

Now you're likely scared for sure!

Don't be, it's not as difficult as it seems, and the benefits to you will help you bypass that ever-expanding waiting line in the hiring process, faster than that 'speed-pass line' for Walt Disney World's most popular rides.

Like your 'Best 25 Seconds of Your Life', your call (and many times, voice mail) needs to be front-loaded with value.

When calling a hiring manager directly, unlike the chance encounter, you have a much more overt purpose:

> **Introducing yourself and your unique value and securing a face-to-face meeting (or scheduled phone meeting), better known as an interview.**

Again, you do not get what you do not ask for, so Ask!

Exercise:

Your assignment is to develop a **25 Second Sales Pitch** about yourself, a script really, which contain the most valuable reasons why you offer something others do not. Here again, look to your proudest achievements, the items you can speak with the most passion about. Don't wait, hesitate, or make excuses, I know you can do this, so pick up your pen...

Follow a structure that is similar to this:

> **Acknowledge them, and introduce yourself by name and ask them how they are this morning.**

And then pause.

Wait for the response to your question about their morning or afternoon. Whether good, bad, or ugly in their response, that part is quite irrelevant.

Just be ready to acknowledge their response, and keep moving on your agenda for the call. If, as an example, they say, "Terrible!" (about their morning), then respond with something confident like,

> **"Well, hopefully that is about to change." ... and move on, without waiting for a further commentary or response.**

If handled professionally on your end, the proper greeting will always buy you a few seconds of listening time on their end, as a courtesy to you. Be sure to greet them using only their first name, and in a tone that you might use with a close and respected friend.

Your precious moment of opportunity has now arrived, so:

> Tell them why you are calling (could be excitement about their company, etc. along with the desire to introduce yourself to them).

Immediately, without pause:

> Tell them your degree accomplishments (schools, if they are notable).

Again, Immediately without delay followed with:

> 2 or 3 key accomplishments with tangibles that you had developed during your Resume Renovation.

Now **Close!**

'Closing':
An all-mysterious sales technique, is simply asking specifically for something that you want and attempting to get agreement on it.

But, what do you want? Should you ask them if they have a need for a person like you on their team? Should you say that you saw a position posted on their website that you are interested in? Well, you could ask either of these or many others. But what you really want, if you think long enough about it, is to be able to meet with them (whether in-person or for a scheduled phone meeting), so you could share more about your background and why you offer what others may not. So, why not just ask for the meeting (don't scare yourself during the call by calling it an 'interview'). It's just a meeting between two valuable individuals within your industry. Sounds like good networking to me, no matter the outcome.

Try this 'Close' to your call:

> **I'm setting up meetings with key individuals in our industry this week and I would like to include you on my schedule. What would work best for your schedule, Jack?**

Granted, that may be a little too direct and aggressive for your style, but I wanted you to know what is possible, and share with you that even this level of directness does work. Along the way, you will find your confidence surely tested, but you will grow immensely through this process, and that will show through in your other work activities - even for your current employer.

Who Ya Gonna Call (there're no ghosts and no reason for fear)

The Boss & The Boss' Boss

As you may recall from earlier, I have a friend that is pursuing a choice job with a major university's communications department. The size of the response to this position being posted is quite overwhelming, and likely in the thousands, since the first three hours of its posting garnered over 600 resumes. The odds do seems daunting. Why even bother applying? Well, because the other choice, just giving up, is not a very palatable one. But fear not, or fear be damned, my friend miraculously has his first face-to-face meeting (that's an interview for those not paying attention), scheduled for this Thursday. No phone-screen, or preliminary interview over the telephone needed. How is that possible, more magic and more luck? It's the culmination of a concerted effort in:

(1.) networking;
(2.) discovering the job opening and responding immediately; and
(3.) delivering extraordinary value in his outreach and communications with them (He reached out to the Boss).

You can make these miracles happen too, by developing yourself as your Self-Recruiter, and following all of the steps in this book. Those steps include the ones that you may be most resistant to trying. Simply calling the boss or the boss's boss will not ensure success. You need to be methodical about every step. Build and develop your sales material -your resume and cover letter, among other possibilities.

Build and work your network (think LinkedIn), and not only apply through HR channels and their dreaded applicant tracking system, but also reach out and engage the boss directly.

Which candidates is the boss most likely to have in their mind when looking over the stacks and stacks of resumes? Would it be one of the other faceless, sometimes headless resumes? Or might the boss be dwelling on the value pieces you were able to convey, when you had reached out to them directly, and be thing of you.

You know what to say to them, we just finished that section, and you have hopefully, put some work into developing your own script by now. So pick up the phone, and make that all important call that helps set you apart from the rest.

You Can Apply, But Don't Submit! (and other stories about control)
When my driver's license was recently expiring, I had to visit one of my least favorite places: the DMV, the Department of Motor Vehicles. The individuals that work there, I'm sure, are nice people just like me. But why when entering the office for my renewal, do I suddenly feel like I have stepped into molasses in the wintertime? Even the smallest move, step or change seems to take place in a frozen time warp. By the time I'm exiting the building, most of the humanity seems to have been drained from my near corpse-like remaining shell of my former self. The answer to all my puzzlement isn't difficult to determine. I had to give up all control to a system that no longer works for the best benefit of all participants, on either side of the process. Same goes for many HR departments and applicant tracking systems. I'm not here to find negative things to say about HR departments or HR professionals - hey, some of my best friends are in HR. And for the most part, they do a great job with the many diverse issues and responsibilities that they have to juggle. However, like the DMV, the larger and more established the department, the greater the likelihood that their systems or their way of handling the interview and application process, has long ago gone off track and, in many cases, it can no longer be called humane.

> **The only way to win,**
> **is to not play the game.**

Change has come, my friend.

> **Reset the rules that you don't like, and stay in control.**

I'm not advising you to alienate anyone that works for a potential future employer. I'm simply advocating that in addition to applying (or submitting, as HR seems to prefer it), you reach out with value directly to the boss, and be sure your message gets heard amongst all the white noise created in any hiring process. This ability with direct outreach will serve you well, whether at this early stage of trying to get the interview or somewhere along the way toward getting your offer.

Don't Be a Stalker, But Call, Call, Call... with Value With a Plan of Attack, You Can be Growing in Value Every Time You Reach Out

So, now you know who, and how to make the call. But, you need to have a strategy for those efforts or your calls may go unnoticed.

Do salespeople call you at work? They call me, but I place salespeople with my clients, as part of my recruiting business, so that would be expected. But I also have other company's salespeople call me trying to sell me on why my business needs to use their product or services. Many don't realize who they are calling, and that they are competing with another great salesperson, right on that call (me). That's okay, just as hiring managers that you reach out to will give you the courtesy few moments of time to express your value, assuming you handle the professional greeting correctly, I also give a few moments of time to those sales individuals that call me. In a way, it is a nice exercise for myself as I read between the lines, analyze their technique and categorize them into various levels of sales ability. I'm never cruel, and I'm always respectful, so they never know it's a real audition call. It's a great built-in laboratory for me, as a recruiter, to have time to exercise my own skills away from my actual sales calls.

What I see more often than not, is that most salespeople call in unprepared to effectively communicate their value.

Many have come to expect getting voice mail, so they often get caught off guard and find themselves scrambling for a recovery when I actually answer the phone in person. That's okay, I have found myself in the same situation on occasion too. We are all only human after all. But, more often than not, I will get repeated calls or voice mails without any change, shift or addition in value, because they did not have a meaningful strategy to build their value with each successive message or contact.

You can, and should be, building your value with every call, message or email that you send.

Now that you have surely completed your resume renovation, you should have developed many great selling points for yourself and your background. Since you are only including 2 or 3 key points on any call or message, so long as you keep track, and strategize on how to make the next message or next call with additional value, unveiling these additional pieces or tidbits will continue to visually solidify your brand in the hiring person's mind.

Remember, your consistent value-filled messaging efforts will work, even when you are calling someone that does not call you back.

Remember my friend with the interview on Thursday? He did reach out to the boss, but as yet, he has not spoken in live conversation with the manager. That does not mean the messaging is not working. His case shows clearly that he was able to develop a clear picture of value in the manager's mind, and that's why he got the call from HR to set up the interview, no real questions asked. So plan ahead, strategize about your message and approach, and call, call, call.

The Best Laid Plans (actually do work, and you can too)

It's a Project, so Track and Manage it like One!

Years ago, when I was a younger, less experienced manager, I was selected to run my company's #4 store in the country, out of about 120 stores at the time. After my hard-fought campaign to communicate my value and demonstrate that I was the right choice to our regional manager, I won the job. Hurray, now the hard work begins. Though I still, in my opinion, was the best choice out of the select group competing for the position, I felt like a grill-cook with an empty propane tank and I was unable to make the kind of progress that I had hoped for within the first few months. What was I missing?

> **A plan for success:**
>
> **An effective plan, and an effective way to track and monitor my plan's progress.**

Eventually, I did achieve the goals that I had set for myself, but it was a learning curve that I wanted to be sure to be ahead of, the next time I faced such a challenge.

We have talked about the importance of controlling your own hiring process, as a Self-Recruiter. This control is more than just trying to control what goes on elsewhere (within HR, with the Hiring Manager, etc.), it's also about controlling and concentrating your efforts with your communications approach and strategy. And it's about setting personal goals for your job search activities (number of companies that you reach out to; number and types of outreach to hiring managers, etc.). It's very easy to not make progress. As when I was a new manager taking on new tasks, it's easy to lose control and stop tracking and assessing the results of your efforts. This is the surest way not to achieve your goals. Dream big, and reach for something difficult and you will likely like the results you will begin to get.

So, make a plan with real tangible goals, such as:

> **"My goal is to identify 3, 6, or 10 new potential opportunities each week."**
>
> **"My goal is to apply to these opportunities (through HR application process)."**

Followed by

> **"My goal is to develop a calling strategy plan and tracking sheet for each new opportunity for which I apply."**
>
> **"My goal is to 'work' each calling strategy plan, by calling, until I have completed all the steps that I have outlined."**
>
> **"My goal is to review each of these tracking sheets every Friday afternoon and assess my successes and missed opportunities."**

With a solid plan and real goals in place, now you'll surely be cooking with gas!

Careful What You Ask For... I booked the Interview, So Now What?

I have to say it again: Congratulations, for making it this far.

> **If you have taken my advice to heart, and put in the appropriate amount of effort, you will have interview opportunities coming your way shortly.**

Managers will always consider potentially adding a sharp individual to their team that can really contribute, even in times of economic uncertainty. Just put your best foot forward, and be sure it represents who you are and who you will be in the potential role.

In a way, we are who we always were, or who we used to be. I was and still am in many ways, that shy individual that I had been, growing up as a child. I learned a very valuable lesson in high school, one that I still carry with me, even today. We are not simply the individual we see within our own minds, we are the individual that others see by judging all the various aspects of ourselves from the outside. It was the summer between my sophomore and junior year of high school where this revelation took place. My family was moving from our long-time residence in Phoenix to a much smaller locale in southwest Florida. The prospect of returning from my Wisconsin summer to a new home, neighborhood and school was, again, something I looked at as a daunting challenge. With a blank slate from which to work, it was not difficult to reinvent myself, even at that age, and before long, I enjoyed a new confidence on the outside, which matched the person I had always known on the inside. Without the weight of the prejudgements of the past, I was able to put my best self, my best foot, forward and so can you.

So, whether you have scheduled that first interview yet, or will do so shortly, what should you do to make the most of the opportunity?

> **All the preparation work and research that you can,**
> **in order to ensure that you have the best chance at success!**

Be sure that research includes all background information and press releases about the company and their products and everything you can find out about individual(s) with which you are to meet. Not only may your HR contact be able to provide you with more information about the manager, you have Google and LinkedIn as resources as well. With the right amount of research and preparation, you'll be off and running, ready to make the most of your interview opportunity.

The Love Connection: Building and Creating the Right Chemistry

Is it really possible to build and create chemistry where none exists? I know that it is.

When I went away to college, I was fortunate to have an apartment with two other bedrooms, besides my own. I advertised the rooms for rent for the school year and, that, in turn, became my monthly living expense funds. I had many different types of individuals that were knocking on my door to look at, and express their interest in, my off-campus housing space. The personalities ran the gamut to say the very least, and I was most focused on my number one priority: which candidates for my potential roommates had the least likelihood of having difficulty getting the rent check in on time. After all, I was counting on that rent for my living expenses. So, I did not choose individuals for many of the usual reasons, ones that I might like as a buddy or a friend. Yet if the time spent over the school year was not going to be uncomfortable, there must be a chemistry fit as well. As roommates over my college years, I had cowboys and farmers, engineers and philosophers, and one guy in law school. He made it in, because I saw him as a 'sure thing' when thinking about my check arriving on time. The year flew by and come May, he had enjoyed living in the space and with myself and my other roommate so well, that he was quick to say that he would like to return for the Fall semester. I'm sure you may have guessed by now, he was my least favorite roommate of all. As a young law student, you might imagine he had his peculiarities, as do we all, but we were not, in the least, a match for roommates. And not for a second time around. Now imagine his surprise when I very nicely and very respectfully let him know that we had not been a good match as roommates, but that I did wish him well for the next semester. He had thought we were like two pigs in a poke or that we would be good friends. I liked him, but no. How was this mastery achieved? Deception? Manipulation? Fraud?

> **No, I simply chose to build chemistry with him and find the areas where we could agree and see eye to eye, so that we could both benefit.**

He had a year in a great apartment and with good, friendly roommates, and I had the security of the check arriving on time. You can build that chemistry too as a Self-Recruiter, even with people you have never met, and I'll show you how.

The simplest way to build chemistry?
Get the other individual to talk about their favorite subject.

What subject might that be? Just look into that mirror, Narcissus. Though everyone may try to deny it is so, most every individual's favorite subject is themselves. No judgements here (I'm too busy with the mirror myself). Understanding this key element of universal personality will serve you well, and give you the ability to create that chemical connection with almost anyone. During the interview process, which is a time of high-anxiety and stress for both participants on either side of the desk, use of this technique will not only help put both the interviewer and the interviewee in a more relaxed and open state, it will help lay a foundation of chemistry on which you can build.

Exercise:

Your challenge:

Have a friend role-play an interview situation with you. Have them take on the manager role, and you, of course, are the candidate coming into their office for the meeting. Ask them to be ready with a few basic interview questions, with the intention to get right down to business and focus on those questions, your answers and so forth.

For this exercise and simplicity of example, let's go with the interviewer being named Jack Smith. Let your friend know that if the discussion turns to them, they are free to talk about their own background as if it were Jack's.

Here we go!

After shaking their hand, sitting in the offered seat, greeting and thanking them professionally for the opportunity to meet with them, and exchanging business cards, your goal is to look for an opening, which may be just a brief moment of pause.

Then, practice jumping right in (almost interrupting them if necessary) with something like this, in a very friendly, engaging and warm tone:

> **"Jack, before we get started, I was curious.
> How long have you been with XYZ Company?"**

The answer may be a short term, and then you could ask:

> **"Oh, out of curiosity,
> where were you before joining XYZ Company?"
> (in a non-judgemental and pleasing tone)**

and maybe continuing with:

> **"How did you like being at (their last employer)?
> (with a smile and a pause)**

If the original answer had been a longer term (with XYZ Company), your follow up question could have been:

> **"Oh, you must like it!?
> (in a non-judgmental and pleasing tone)(long pause afterward)**

What we are doing is giving them an opening to their favorite subject, themselves.

> **It may take just one gentle warm question or**
> **it may take a couple or several.**

But before long they will be off and running about themselves and the tension in the room, for both of you, will have relaxed as the chemistry has started to form.

> **It simple really:**

> **Just be genuine (I really do have a real and genuine interest in finding out more about them, after all, we may be working together shortly) and show interest in the other person and truly listen.**

Now, that's always a welcomed trait that can bring out the Narcissus in us all.

Love Letter to Yourself:
Thank You Notes that Solve Your Problems in Advance

You may recall my campaign to communicate my value as a young manager interviewing with my company for a store manager position running one of their top locations. Even though I had not achieved this level inside a company as large as that employer yet, I thought that I had done everything necessary so that they would see my value clearly when comparing me to the other candidates, but I made a junior-level mistake in my meeting. They had been very impressed, as they had not met another individual during the interview process with the command of language and conversation which I had demonstrated. I thought I was a shoe-in for the spot. A little birdie on the inside (always a very good idea to be working your network) alerted me to the fact that I had not effectively made my case, and that, in fact they were arguing and discussing whether I was ready for the position, right at that moment. What did I miss? I had not clearly articulated my vision for the store, should I be selected. That missing vision probably went hand in hand with the missing plan of action that I had mentioned to you earlier. Luckily, I had not yet sent out my thank you note. In that note I recounted my enthusiasm for the position, for the opportunity to contribute more, and noted that I may not have spent enough of my focus during our meeting on how I intended to move the store to the next level. I welcomed an opportunity to meet with them again, if they would like to discuss that aspect further. They did not take me up on the offer, but I did get the job.

Your thank you notes can be your salvation as well.

They are a requirement if you are to differentiate yourself from the other individuals that you are competing against. Frankly, most people today completely drop the ball on thank you notes. That makes it even easier for you to be able to be a stand out.

After the interview, ask yourself one simple question:

"If I am not selected for the position, or not selected to move forward, what would the reason be?"

This question is another tool for your Self-Recruiter toolkit. Simple as it seems, the question's structure will shine that florescent light on potential mistakes or omissions which may have occurred during your interview. Learn to trust whatever pops into your head as the answer, as in almost every case you will have a bulls-eye marking the hiring individual's greatest concern. Don't stop asking until you have an answer. If none 'pops', then make up an answer. Yes, I said make up an answer. By doing so, you will be nurturing your own self-diagnostic ability and refining your Self-Recruiter skills. More often that not, you will be right on target.

Now, for whatever weakness that you shine that light upon, weave a word or two into your thank you note and offer to discuss that area further.

It is scary to point out a potential weakness, usually one that we have no desire to discuss, especially during an interview process. The reality is that it's more about demonstrating your perceptiveness and that will go a long way to solving any concerns about the issue in advance.

Send an email thank you shortly after the interview (shortly, but certainly within 2 hours, at the most, for greatest impact) and get to the post office before five p.m. with a simple, hand written, thank you card which will reinforce your specialness when it arrives the next day.

Don't Get Caught with Your Pants Down: Be Prepared for the Unexpected

As recruiters, we do love to share our war stories as a way to inspire and motivate one another about preparation and its importance at every step in the interview process. One such recruiter, when asked about his experiences, shared one that I find quite memorable. He had a candidate set up for an interview with one of his best client companies. He had briefed and prepared his candidate for the interview, much like you will be doing shortly, for yourselves, with your new-found Self-Recruiter skills, and he thought that everything had been covered. The candidate, taking all of the advice to heart, made sure that he arrived at the company's location early, as recommended, but in heading the warning to also be respectful of the manager's time by not actually showing up in the office more that five minutes early, he decided to just park and wait in his car for the appropriate time. Well, as the time kept ticking and it was still too early, the candidate found himself in need of a restroom after consuming an extra large coffee during the trip to the interview location. What to do, what to do. This individual decided, in his infinite wisdom, to honor the advice of not showing up too early by exiting his vehicle, walking into the nearby woods and relieving himself on a tree. All the while, the manager had been looking out the window in anticipation of the potential candidate's arrival. And, you guessed it, the manager was treated to much more of a show than he had bargained for. I can tell you that this candidate did not get the job offer, what I cannot tell you is whether the manager shook the candidate's hand.

The unexpected can, and usually does, happen during the interview process.

It could take the form of the manager receiving a call in the middle of your interview, throwing his feet up on the desk, shouting and arguing with whomever may be on the other end of the phone. It could take the form of meeting with three different individuals, when you had been told you would be meeting with just one. Or it could be something more colorful, such as in the recruiter's war story.

You must prepare for the unexpected if you are to avoid the bumps and pitfalls along the way to your next career opportunity.

This also means having multiple extra copies of your resume handy in case you are introduced to a number of individuals, rather than the one that you had expected. You must be cognizant of your body language, and what it communicates, at all times and not become to casual while a manager takes a moment from your interview time to get side tracked in some way. And you have to balance all the advice and recommendations with personal common sense and make the right choice to go into a building's lobby to use the restroom, should the need arise. While it may seem impossible to prepare for every situation, the more contingencies you do plan for, the less likely it will be that you will be memorable for the wrong reasons.

Don't Talk About Money!

Getting Your Best Offer: Salary & Benefits

Would you like more money? I know I would. That question is another one of mine which I always ask, when teaching seminars on negotiating. I simply single-out several people in my audience, one by one, putting them on the spot and I challenge them with a demanding and resonating tone, "Do you want more money?" It's a great parlor trick, of sorts, to elicit some communal pressure that will make it more difficult for the individual to be honest. Our society, while loving money, looks down on anyone that says they love money. Yet, even with the group dynamic and the societal disapproval, virtually everyone I do ask, eventually musters the courage to admit... that they would like more money. And there is absolutely nothing wrong with that, assuming you have not taken a vow of poverty.

> **So, as a strong performer and sharp candidate,**
> **it's okay for you to want more money as well,**
> **just don't ask for it, and don't talk about money at all.**

Now there's an enigma.

We want, but must not ask for, more money. But then, how do we get more money? For the answer, just look to one of the oldest dilemmas for the modern couple: the choice of engagement ring. Whether you were the giver or receiver of that ring is irrelevant, what I'm looking at is the dynamic surrounding the choice of the ring's most precious focus, the diamond. Though over the years this focus has come to be discussed much more openly between couples, rest assured a disappointing choice by the future husband-to-be for too little pain in the short-term with respect to this decision, could set off an earthquake of response, especially from the bride-to-be's friends, threatening the couple's very foundation. It's a symbol of love. It's, rightly or wrongly, one measure of the love. Too little love, and the rest of the foundation for the relationship can be called into question. Luckily for those that have chosen incorrectly, love also can conquer all, and these days, many stores will do the same and facilitate the necessary exchange, especially to a more expensive ring. And, let's not forget, love is an endless well of forgiveness, even for the unforgivable.

In our quest for more money, all we really have to do is not talk about it, for the most part. Many of the individuals that I place as a recruiter, are sales professionals of some sort. I could probably not find another group that is more obsessed with money, and rightly so since their entire livelihood is focussed on the movement of money (and product) as a major element of their day to day activities. As candidates for a potential position, they have a very difficult time not focussing and thinking about money, almost to a distracting level.

> **My advice to you is the same as my advice to them: Get over it!**
>
> **During any stage of the interview process, if you want to receive the best possible offer, one that does not leave unclaimed money on the table, avoid the subject of money and compensation like the plague.**

We may be interested in whether the plague has arrived down the street or even next door, but in the case of money, put on those blinders.

The pitfalls, there are always a few.
Beware the stack of papers that will be handed to you at some point when

meeting with an HR representative. The question that 'dare not speak its name' is right in there, and you mustn't answer, no matter how strong your desire to, no matter what.

> **"What is your expected or desired salary?"**

No, nada, never, bite your tongue, and hold your pen! Simply write, "Open." or "To be discussed." End of discussion. Put too high a figure, and you don't get the interview or the next round. Put too low a figure, and you'll never get the job or you may walk away from an offer because you feel insulted (which might be a little unfair, since you gave them the number in the first place). Here again, the only way to win, is to not play the game. Or at least, to play the game my way.

> **Love, that's how you get the right diamond.**
> **Love, that's how you get the right money or compensation as well.**

As I had said, love conquers all, so trust that it will in your case. You should be spending your energies throughout the interview process building the chemistry, strengthening the foundation, and showing how your value exceeds all others.

Let them fall in love with you, as the most valuable addition to their team. After all, that is exactly why they will eventually choose you for the role, if you have done the appropriate amount of work to get lucky.

The Unwelcome Truth: To Be Loved and Taken For Granted

They love me, but my offer is still too low!

An individual that I had been working with to place with one of my clients, worked for a major university in Atlanta. He was in information technology and he had a great education to go along with his skill-sets. He was an 'A+' in his field. He had been with his current employer for nine years, during which time he had seen a number of his colleagues, his equals, go on to another company, two, or even three, and they were now earning much more than he was receiving in his compensation. He could no longer reconcile any reasoning for staying with his employer, and not getting 'his proper share' of the pie. At the time, he was earning $65,000. His former colleagues were now earning between $85,000. and $95,000. You can imagine his emotions about this, which might be natural. When a company puts together an offer, they do not simply look at the position and say, "Anyone that I hire for this role gets 'X' dollars." It's typically a range of potential salaries, and that range can be rather large sometimes. The 'unwelcome truth' is what usually determines what you may be offered.

The Unwelcome Truth:

Companies usually pay, and base their potential offers, on your pay history.

In my candidate's case, maybe staying with his current employer for the last nine years, while colleagues of his had been moving up the ladder with strategic moves in two or three companies, may not have been the best long-term choice.

No matter, you cannot look to, or expect the new employer to pay for the 'sins' of the past employer (taking advantage of you and not paying you what might have been the going market rates).

He had a difficult choice to make: stay with his current employer and let the pay discrepancy continue to grow exponentially, or move to a new employer for a reasonable increase, and be taken advantage of in a new place. Of course, staying involved by actively managing your career path, will help you avoid ending up in an extreme case like his. But, what about when you have stayed involved, followed the Self-Recruiter advice and still received an unpleasant jolt of reality when getting an offer that may be different and not quite what you had expected?

Sometimes, no matter how correctly you have handled all the various aspects of your interview process, and even when successfully avoiding the 'Expected/Desired Salary' question, something goes wrong unexpectedly. That's okay, as I'm sure you are planning ahead for the unexpected by now as a new Self-Recruiter. Let's roll up our sleeves and get right down to it.

In this example, let's look at an individual that is currently earning $65,000. They have just received their offer, having followed most all of my advice as a good Self-Recruiter. They also had reasonable expectations of increasing their salary by $6500. to a base of $71,500. Why do I suggest that that is a reasonable increase? Well, in most cases, that's a reasonable percentage, 8 - 10%, that a good candidate can expect when changing jobs, assuming that they have successfully convinced the hiring manager of their value. Yes, on occasion, I've seen 15%, 20% and even an astounding 30%, but those cases are very rare.

If your offer is in a reasonable range, my recommendation to you would be to accept it, and not gamble or potentially jeopardize it by having it withdrawn by the company.

But, if it is outside of what you could reasonable expect, and not a figure that you willing to accept, then you may want to consider asking them for more.

Just always go in with your eyes open, and realize that you may end up with no offer at all, especially if not handled correctly, with tact, reason and respect.

Approach the manager and begin by reaffirming your excitement for the role, your commitment to the manager's team, and how much you are looking forward to contributing to the company's bottom line. These main points are why you were selected, and they are a demonstration of your 'love'. Assuming that you have also been successful in making them fall in love with you for the role, they will be more apt to try and solve the point of difficulty that you are about to put worth. You will need to make a good 'case' as to why you should receive more - and just because you stayed too long and feel underpaid by your last employer, will not fly here. Look for opportunities when making your case, which could be your expanding family's financial needs, kid's college tuition and expenses just being down the road, or whatever real and realistic reasons that you focus in on.

Use language and phrases, like:

"I'm just trying to keep myself/my family financially whole."
"I owe it to my family."

Be sure to include (and then to deliver, when you work for the company) value with:

> **"I want to be sure I can contribute the maximum to your team and not be struggling and distracted by being weighed down with financial concerns."**

And again, as needed:

> **"I'm really just trying to keep myself/my family financially whole."**

In the end, if they do come through with the extra needed compensation, remember, this is not a game. Be genuine and genuinely thankful and let them know how much you appreciate it, and how much your family appreciates it. My family, at times that would include myself and my tiger fish, certain appreciate my own efforts.

Ask, Ask Ask, for the Job

By now, your Self-Recruiter toolkit contains many tangible and actionable pieces of value which will be at your disposal, if you use this guide effectively, while searching for your next position. A key theme of this book and a focus of many of its efforts, is to not only put those tools close at hand and at your disposal, it's about turning yourself into a self-advisor and self-counselor, an advisor and counselor just like one of the many very good recruiters in your industry or niche. For this, you need distance from yourself, along with trust in yourself.

As a hiring manager over the years in a number of businesses, I have interviewed many individuals at various levels in their careers. The way a recruiter, or Self-Recruiter in your case, conducts an interview may seem very similar to the way a manager does, but there are key differences. The manager is thinking about you and evaluating you as a potential addition to their team.

> **The recruiter or Self-Recruiter's goals are different for the interview because they are not only thinking of the same aspects that a hiring manager would be thinking about, they are also considering how to better position themselves, at every step in the process, against the competition that they do not get a chance to see: the other candidates competing for the hiring manager's attention.**

Many of the individuals that I work with are the best-of-the-best in their fields. As you might expect, many of them know this fact about themselves. And, since they are usually in sales-related roles, it's not unusual for them to be very confident and sometimes even cocky. That's okay, and not such a bad trait for a successful sales individual. But that self exaltation can work against them, as many times they have difficulty creating 'space' between the reality of who they are as an outstanding and accomplished salesperson in their area of specialty, and who they are as a potential candidate with flaws (we all have them) competing with other top performers for that next great career opportunity.

One heartbreaking example is one from a few years ago when I was working to place one such top performer. This individual was in a very sweet spot with regard to their set of skills and with the demand for those skills being at an all time high. Naturally, they fell into a trap that any top performer can make a misstep into: they were too full of themselves. To properly frame the story, you need to understand just how 'good' they were. This individual was what recruiters call a 'walking invoice'.

In simplest terms, it means they had nearly everything a recruiter, and potential hiring manager, might look for:

- **a solid education;**
- **tremendous and valuable skill-set;**
- **a very nice career progression;**
- **noted and specific tangible accomplishments,**
- **and they were motived to change jobs.**

They also had a vastly over-inflated sense of what their value might be on the market when considering what companies might offer, should they be hired. As much as I tried engaging and coaching the individual trying to persuade them to remain cognizant of the fact that they had other top individuals with which they were completing, they remained convinced that their value would simply overwhelm all other concerns or issues ensuring that the choice would ultimately be theirs.

> **The critical misstep was that in their self-absorbed state, they just assumed the manager would 'know' they wanted the job.**

They were too reserved with their interest, and even aloof, from the very first round of interviews. Their interest and excitement for the potential role did grow through the process, and by the end, they were just beginning to heed some of my advice. But that change in their openness came too late and at a heavy price for them, as an offer was never forthcoming to them after the final round of meetings.

> **See, no matter how good or potentially valuable you may be, there are always others of equal or greater value that are out there too.**

Managers see many individuals and narrow the field down to a select few top performers from which to choose. The candidate had always assumed that they were the best, and they may have been, except for their level of interest and attitude along the way. They never said, "I want the job."

> **At each stage of the interview process, you must be evaluating whether or not this opportunity, this company and this manager are the right fit for you.**

But, do not show your side of the evaluation process to the manager.

Just answer this simple question of yourself:

> **"Am I interested by what I see, and hear, and do I want to hear more?"**

Note that the question did not say, "Do you want the job?" You may not have enough information yet to determine that.

Whether it's your first meeting or phone call about the potential opportunity, or your forth round interview that is getting close to an offer stage, at each and every step, you must look for an opportunity to say something similar to:

> **"Wow, I'm excited by what I'm hearing and I'm very interested. What's our next step?"**

This is true, if your answer to the first question was 'yes'. Imagine and visualize the meetings taking place at the company after each round of interviews is completed. Managers and team members sitting around a table looking over resumes, interview notes, and even the rare thank you note, which may have arrived. Who will be the stand-out in their discussions and in their minds? One of the several random top performers that they are considering or the individual that connected, engaged, and expressed interest at every stage of their interviews?

> **In the end, the goal is to have the choice for yourself.**

Getting that offer allows you to remain in control about the choice, otherwise, you may end up heartbroken when the offer goes to someone else.

In Comedy, It's All About Timing: Be Ready to Accept an Offer on the Spot

In college, I was lucky enough to be cast in a show my first time auditioning, without any completed acting courses or experiences whatsoever. In fact, I wasn't even there to audition. I was there as part of an acting course that I had gotten up the nerve to take and it was only the first week. Mortified and with no monologue with which to dazzle the director, I was singled out, since I was nearly the only one not auditioning, and told to get up there anyway. After a torturous minute and a half on stage introducing myself and saying a few words, it seemed more like a self flagellation scene from the Da Vinci Code, rather than something that I would call a success.

Of course, I got lucky. I was just a little older than many of those auditioning, and the role for which I was cast was well-suited to my physical look. And then, just like in a Fame flashback, my name appeared later in the week on the notice board of parts that had been given out - to the sneers and jeers of those who did not get cast and who would be surely waiting in the wings for me to fall on my face. As excited as I was to have the part, I was petrified. See, it was a comedy. No one had ever said to me that I was funny. I had never, ever told a joke successfully. Worse than that, it was a British farce, accents and all. No small challenge indeed. Little did I know at that point in my life, but you don't have to be funny to be funny. My salvation was in my determination to really become the character. He wasn't funny at all, he was serious and absurd. He was supposed to be a second-string character of not that much importance. But in my hands, he apparently became very funny to the audience, as well as to the state theatre auditors, and I received one of the only two acting awards given by them for the show. It was about timing. I could be the 'straight man' and the timing determined the success or failure, the emotional fulfillment, and the audience's enjoyment.

Timing in the interview process can be equally important.

Just a slight misstep on either side with regard to a number of issues, and one party or the other may get their feelings hurt, or worse, somehow feel insulted. The results of this kind of misstep can be dramatic. You could find yourself not making the next round of the interview process, not receiving an offer at all, or it could cause a manager to rethink their choice of you for the role, even though the offer has already been extended.

> **While there are many areas these missteps could happen throughout the process, the most important with regards to timing is the moment of the offer being extended to you.**

Think about it from the manager's perspective. If the manager has conducted a thorough and lengthy interview process, narrowed down a larger pool of individuals to just a talented few, conducted at length multi-level interviews along the way, and made the decision that you were that 'right one' with your skills and enthusiasm to welcome to the team, how would you feel, as the manager, if the person said,

> **"Great, I would like to think about it."**

It may be very reasonable to have time to consider and think about an offer, but in every second of time after the offer has been extended, the doubt is beginning to creep in. Tick, tick, tick.

The manager thinks,

> **"Did I make the right choice?"**
> **"I thought the candidate wanted it?"**
> **"Maybe I should have gone with my close second."**

Before long, that offer containing a generous date before expiration, can be withdrawn and evaporate like an audience's attention to a comedy that is just not funny.

As you get close to receiving your offer, you should be sitting down, in advance, and having important discussions with whomever may also be involved in your decision-making process - be it another-half, your spouse, or a close friend whom you may turn to for counsel.

You don't need to wait for the piece of paper, the offer, to make your decision on whether to accept or not.

By now, your HR contact should have already spoken to you during the process about the benefits and such that are available to employees.

The only real mystery is likely the number: What number (salary and various compensation pieces) will they offer you.

Being a sharp individual that has made it to this point where you are likely to be receiving an offer shortly, make up several numbers for yourself. Realistic please, it's not the time for pie-in-the-sky. Yes, we all want the most we can get, so I'm sure you'll be ready for additional negotiations, based on my advice from earlier, if the offer is a 'miss' somehow.

But for now, come up with three reasonable choices on your part about what that 'number' might be.

Now talk with your trusted confidant and make your decision for each number, as if it had been offered to you.

Just choose wisely, and don't play a game just to try to get more, because your timing might cause the manager to look to the candidates that are surely waiting in the wings. And that would not be funny at all.

LIFTOFF

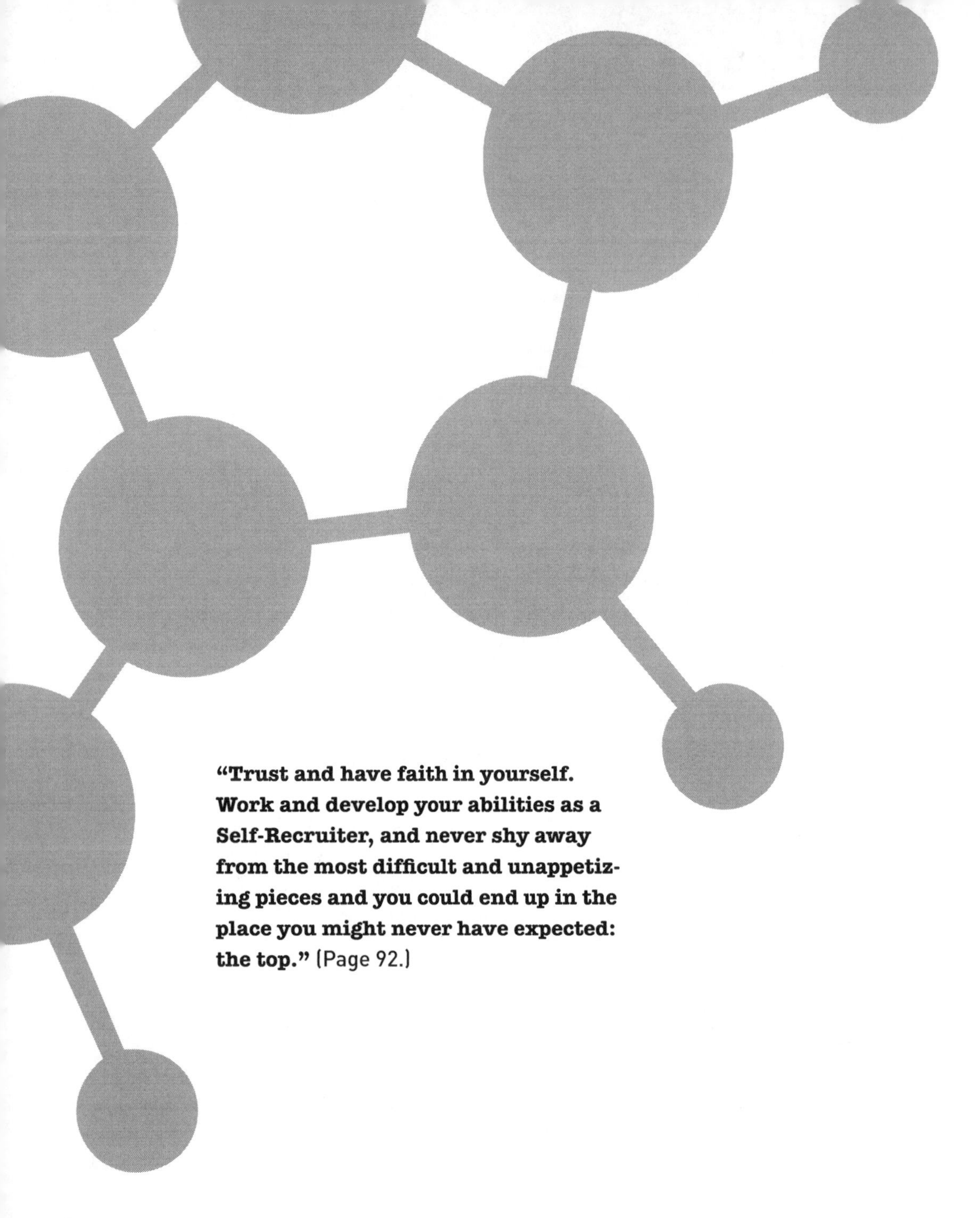

"Trust and have faith in yourself. Work and develop your abilities as a Self-Recruiter, and never shy away from the most difficult and unappetizing pieces and you could end up in the place you might never have expected: the top." (Page 92.)

LIFTOFF

I Can't Really Do This Can I?
Nice Attitude, That Will Get You Places
(that you don't want to be)

Our natural traits of questioning and doubting ourselves can help us avoid one of the major things we face in life: risk. That risk-avoidance can be a lifesaver. It keeps us from some of the dangers of the world that could be our undoing. It keeps us from getting too close to a cliff's edge. It can help us make the choice for taking a well lit street, rather than the shortcut through the dark alley. It keeps us from coming face to face with some of our worst fears. But those traits, while very useful at times- especially when evaluating our steps and choices as a Self-Recruiter, will also hold us back when taking on a new and challenging role for ourselves as advisor, counselor, and motivator in the Self-Recruiter process. Yes, we need to question and doubt at every step of the way to be sure that our selections and choices allow for the best possible chance of success.

But we mustn't allow that questioning and doubt to erode our fortitude for taking on the daunting challenges set forth by this book.

Though I did not overly challenge myself with sports and those kinds of competitions as a child, once out in the world, I did discover a strong love for the outdoors. I grew to love camping and hiking and just getting away from it all in nature. It's a wonderful antidote to what ails in the modern world. One of my favorite places to visit is Yosemite. If you have not made it there for a visit, it must be added to your list of must-sees. Though a much larger park than most people think, the area most people visualize and associate with Yosemite is just a small valley within the park. It has a single road in, which loops the valley and, when done with your visit, it loops you back out through the same tunnel which is cut straight through the mountain. Be forewarned, the area of roadway just after exiting the tunnel and entering the valley is one that is home to many a fender-bender. The view is so astounding and unexpected to our minds, that many a driver has seemed to have forgotten that they are still behind the wheel driving a vehicle and, well you can imagine the results. When standing there on the valley floor, which is only about a mile wide, though several miles long, you are surrounded on three sides by nearly sheer cliffs rising a mile or more straight upward. The trees are enormously tall, yet seem like miniatures on a model against the backdrop of the sights and waterfalls rising toward the heavens. It really does look like a painting or artificial backdrop that might be found in a photo studio somewhere, especially once you step into the shot.

A quick Google search will return many pictures with the valley's most prominent features. The most photographed of which is probably a massive, sold monolith of granite, sheered off on one side, appropriately named Half Dome. My favorite camp area sits near the back of the valley at its base and next to the winding river. It's an inspiring and awesome sight to behold. Since my very first visit, I had such a strong desire to be one of the relatively few that made it all the way to the top. Over 8,800 feet high, and directly above my campsite. In order to get there, you have to hike about nine miles each way, and that was thousands of feet going up, and thousands of feet coming back down. No supplies, food, water or porta-potties along the way. But, who was I kidding, I was not 'that kind' of outdoor guy. I think it was on my third visit where I undertook this challenge. It involved overcoming many a warning stating that the average person could never accomplish this feat in a single day and must plan for camping in the wilderness en route along the way, if they were to be successful. It also involved ignoring the warnings of bears and mountain lions in the area meant to trigger the risk-avoidance in us all. And, of course, those animals are really there, it's their habitat after all. If you ever doubt that point, the park service has a nice display of a car with its windows smashed out and its door ripped off by a hungry local that had spotted a cooler of food sitting on the back seat, instead of in the bear-proof storage lockers, as recommended.

Fear can be a wonderful thing.

It can be a great motivator to be our best selves (thanks again, Jack) or it can keep us from achieving our goals.

Determined to achieve my goal, I did all the research and planning that I could do. I concluded that to make it in a single day and arrive back at my campsite before sunset, I would need to head out at about four in the morning, in the dark. Until you actually try hiking and climbing all those thousands of feet over the course of nine miles toward some goal, you really can't be prepared for just how taxing and strenuous that it can be. So yes, I had unbelievable burning sensations throughout my body for the next 13 hours that my round trip ended up taking. I had decided that I was going to make it, or quite possibly, die trying. Once you focus in on that kind of determination, you will be amazed at what that focus will help you achieve.

Maybe because of just how difficult I expected the journey to be, along with how determined I was, it ended up being easier than expected to near the base, and the final 900 feet, of my challenge to the top of Half Dome. As I grew closer and closer to the base, the close-up of the Dome finally came into view. My heart nearly stopped as if facing a precipice on the edge of eternity, for the last of the challenge was a near vertical assent. Its surface is smooth with nothing to hang onto. The park service had drilled holes deep into the rock's face and every Spring they insert long poles into the side of Half Dome and connect them together with a steel cable forming some sort of pathway and last-ditch attempt at safety. Every few feet of assent, you will find a small two-by-four nailed into the smooth surface of the rock in an effort to somehow allow your boots to dig in and hang on.

After putting on the prerequisite leather gloves to protect against the steel cables, I began my four appendage climb. If you are to make it more than a few feet, you must climb with both your legs and your arms in a very coordinated effort. Did I mention yet that this path, carrying what had appeared from only a slight distance away to be ants moving upward, and which was now disappearing over the ever-so-slightly curved slope above -was intended for two way traffic!? One slip, one false step and not only would my goal be dashed. Half way up this monster I had found myself actually crouched with my feet firmly residing on the side of one of those poles sticking out from the granite, my arms clinging to the steel cable now just above my head, and with my eyes closed recounting the wonders of my life as my heart pounded in pain within my chest. Breath. Breath. Breath. I thought about loosening one hand to reach into a pocket for an anti-anxiety pill. Maybe not, probably not a good idea to be relaxed when my life is in danger. I had accomplished and done most of what I had set out to do: I was on Half Dome, if not at its top. As evidenced by my death grip on the cable at that moment, I surely had in fact risked my very life to achieve my dream. I could just slip back down and still hold my head up high. But with nothing more to lose, I mustered the strength of character and might and forced my way against the rock to its very top. It was like the explosion of energy from within the sun. Shaking violently, crying tears of joy, wanting to throw up, and truly feeling what it means to be alive for the first time in my life, I knew that nothing ever again could stop me.

> **The challenges I have laid down for you in this book may be equally scary to you.**

Trust and have faith in yourself. Work and develop your abilities as a Self-Recruiter, and never shy away from the most difficult and unappetizing pieces, and you could end up in the place you might never have expected: the top.

Congratulations again, and now get to work!

RESOURCES

Download this form, and others free at
www.SelfRecruiter.com

SELF RECRUITER®
Changing the Rules:

Tools: **Job Search Activity Goals & Master Tracking Sheet**

Job Titles I'm Looking for:

Start Date of Plan: / /

Self Review of Plan (Every Friday):

	Week 1	Week 2	Week 3	Week 4	Week 5	Week 6	Week 7	Week 8
# of Companies contacted this week:								
# of Emails (outbound):								
# of Calls (outbound):								
# of Calls to Managers:								
# of Calls to HR:								
# of Meaningful Conversations:								
Rate Your Efforts / Week's Results: (1-10 Rating)								

My Job Search Weekly Goals Are:

# of Companies I will contact:

# of Emails (outbound to Managers, or HR):

# of Calls (Total outbound):

# of Calls to Managers:

# of Calls to HR:

# of Meaningful Conversations:

PROVIDENT RESOURCE

Download this form, and others free at
www.SelfRecruiter.com

Tools: **Networking Strategy Sheet Tracking**

Job Opportunity Networking Activity:

On this form, tack **every outreach** (call, message or email) that takes place **between you and a Networking Contact** you may know or uncover.

Be sure to **Note the Strategy / Goal** of each outreach.
(without a specific goal, you are less likely to achieve something with this effort)

When Networking, be sure to think of people in your **Rolodex** and **address book**, on social-networking sites, such as **Facebook**, on professional networking sites such as **LinkedIn**, and those that may be in associations you may also be a member of and any organization of professionals for your niche.

Date	Who	Strategy for Message / Dialogue	Results	Linked in LinkedIN?
				Y N
				Y N
				Y N
				Y N
				Y N
				Y N
				Y N
				Y N
				Y N
				Y N
				Y N
				Y N
				Y N
				Y N
				Y N
				Y N
				Y N
				Y N
				Y N
				Y N
				Y N
				Y N
				Y N
				Y N
				Y N
				Y N
				Y N

PROVIDENT RESOURCE

Download this Form, and others Free at www.SelfRecruiter.com

Download this form, and others free at
www.SelfRecruiter.com

Tools: **Resumes Sent Activity Tracking Sheet**

Job Titles I'm Looking for:

On this form, tack **every resume sent during your job search process** (email response to ads, direct emails to hiring managers, snail mail) that takes place **from you to a company or individual** you may be interested in developing as an opportunity.

Be sure to **Note the Target / Goal** for each resume sent.
(without a specific goal, you are less likely to achieve something with this effort)

Date	Sent To (Company)	Sent To (Contact)	By Direct Email / HR System / Mail	Results (Date)	Follow Up Steps?
			Email HR-S Mail		
			Email HR-S Mail		
			Email HR-S Mail		
			Email HR-S Mail		
			Email HR-S Mail		
			Email HR-S Mail		
			Email HR-S Mail		
			Email HR-S Mail		
			Email HR-S Mail		
			Email HR-S Mail		
			Email HR-S Mail		
			Email HR-S Mail		
			Email HR-S Mail		
			Email HR-S Mail		

PROVIDENT RESOURCE

Download this Form, and others Free at www.SelfRecruiter.com

Download this form, and others free at
www.SelfRecruiter.com

SELF RECRUITER®
Changing the Rules:

Tools: **30 Second Calling Script**

Job Opportunity Title:

Company: | **Phone / Email**

Hiring Manager(s):

HR Contact(s):

Follow a structure that is similar to this:

Acknowledge them, and introduce yourself by name and ask them how they are this morning, etc.

And then pause:

Wait for the response to your question about their morning or afternoon. Whether good, bad, or ugly in their response, that part is quite irrelevant.

Just **be ready to acknowledge their response**, and keep moving on your agenda for the call. If, as an example, they say,

"Terrible!" [about their morning], then respond with something confident like,

"Well, hopefully that is about to change." ... **and move on, without waiting for a further commentary or response**

Tell them why you are calling [could be excitement about their company, etc. along with the desire to introduce yourself to them].

Immediately, without pause:

Tell them your degree accomplishments [schools, if they are notable].

Again, Immediately without delay followed with:

2 or 3 key accomplishments with tangibles that you had developed during your ***Resume Renovation***.

Now Close!
[Ask for what you would like: An Interview or to Schedule a Phone Meeting with you]

Greet Them

(wait for response)

Acknowledge Their Response

Tell Them Why You Are Calling

Your Educational Background

2 or 3 Key Accomplishments

Close

PROVIDENT RESOURCE

Download this Form, and others Free at www.SelfRecruiter.com

Download this form, and others free at
www.SelfRecruiter.com

SELF RECRUITER®
Changing the Rules:

Tools:

Calling Strategy Sheet
Company Tracking

Job Opportunity Title:

Phone / Email

Company:

Hiring Manager(s):

HR Contact(s):

On this form, tack **every outreach** (call, message or email) that takes place **between you and a company** you may be interested in.

Be sure to **Note the Strategy / Goal** of each outreach.
(without a specific goal, you are less likely to achieve something with this effort)

Date	Who	Strategy for Message / Dialogue	Results

PROVIDENT RESOURCE

Download this form, and others free at
www.SelfRecruiter.com

SELF RECRUITER®
Changing the Rules:

Tools: **Interview Strategy Sheet**
Opportunity Tracking

Job Opportunity Title:

Res

Phone / Email

Company:

Hiring Manager(s):

HR Contact(s):

On this form, tack **every stage of the Interview process** (telephone interview(s), face-to-face interview(s) and video conference interview(s)) that takes place **between you and one company** you may be interested in.

Be sure to **Note the Strategy / Goal** of each Interview.

Date	Who	Type	Strategy for Interview	Results / Next Steps

Download this Form, and others Free at www.SelfRecruiter.com

PROVIDENT RESOURCE

Download this form, and others free at
www.SelfRecruiter.com

SELF RECRUITER®
Changing the Rules:

Tools: **Tools Checklist**

Job Titles I'm Looking for:

Start Date of Plan: / /

Self Review of Self-Recruiter Tools

- Florescent-lighting test (P. 9) ☐
- Image-Mind Control (P. 18) ☐
- Resume Definition (P. 21) ☐
- Resume Goals (P. 23) ☐
- Understanding Stacks (P. 23) ☐
- 3 to 5 Seconds (P. 24) ☐
- 3 Second Test (P. 25) ☐
- Work Pedigree (P. 27) ☐
- 3 Keys to Value (P. 28) ☐
- .EDU Review (P. 29) ☐
- Resume Design (P. 32) ☐
- 'Sales' Brochures (P. 37) ☐
- Applicant Tracking Systems (P. 39) ☐
- PDF (P. 41) ☐
- A Word Please (P. 42) ☐
- Best 25 Seconds of Your Life (P. 46) ☐
- Elevator Test (P. 49) ☐
- 25 Second Role-Play (P. 51) ☐
- Whom to Call (P. 53) ☐
- Applying without Submitting (P. 55) ☐
- Plan for Value (P. 56) ☐
- Manage Your Project (P. 58) ☐
- Goal Setting (P. 59) ☐
- Get Ready for the Interview (P. 60) ☐
- Building Chemistry (P. 61) ☐
- Chemistry Role-Play (P. 63) ☐
- About that Thank You Note (P. 65) ☐
- The Key Post-Interview Question (P. 66) ☐
- Planning for the Unexpected (P. 68) ☐
- Getting the Best Offer (P. 70) ☐
- The HR Question to Avoid (P. 72) ☐
- The Unwelcome Truth (P. 73) ☐
- If You Don't Ask (P. 76) ☐
- Timing to Win (P. 80) ☐
- Getting Motivated for Your Search (P. 87) ☐
- Downloaded Self-Recruiter Forms? ☐

PROVIDENT RESOURCE

Download this Form, and others Free at www.SelfRecruiter.com

GLOSSARY OF IMPORTANT TERMS AND PHRASES

A Resume

What is it? It is, and should be, that simple 'Sales Sheet' on a hot product that you want to help create that 'desire' for, that we had talked about.

Resume Goal

A clean, clear, and straightforward format. A format where the information jumps off of the page for the reader. Specific items and accomplishments are included thought to be of greatest interest to the hiring manager, formatted in such a way so they can be easily absorbed at first glance. And, a clear accounting of your educational background and any ongoing training which may be relevant.

Resume's Job

Your resume's job is to 'awaken' the desire of the potential employer to want to hear more, and specifically not to satisfy all of their hunger for knowledge about you.

PDF

which stands for Portable Document Format, is just that. It's a format where almost any document, generated by almost any piece of software, from almost any operating system, can look and print just as great, whether sent down the street or across the globe.

Building Chemistry (The simplest way to build chemistry?)

Get the other individual to talk about their favorite subject.

Self-Recruiter's Goals

are different for the interview, because they are not only thinking of the same aspects that a hiring manager would be thinking about, they are also considering how to better position themselves, at every step in the process, against the competition that they do not get a chance to see: the other candidates competing for the hiring manager's attention.

Closing

An all-mysterious sales technique, is simply asking specifically for something that you want and attempting to get agreement on it.

The Unwelcome Truth

Companies usually pay, and base their potential offers, on your pay history.

A Plan for Success

An effective plan, and an effective way to track and monitor your plan's progress.

Self-Recruiter

An accomplished, confident individual that has taken the reins of control back from others by nurturing their own brand, developing their career plan and goals, and then drives their own hiring process by effectively using and utilizing all the tool in the Self-Recruiter took kit.

INDEX

View of the author and Yosemite Valley from the top, after conquering, his Half Dome challenge.

An avid outdoorsman, the author revels in testing our natural traits of self-questioning and doubting that can usually help us avoid one of the major things we face in life: risk. But without risk, there is little reward.

Yes, we do need to question and doubt at every step of the way to be sure that our selections and choices allow for the best possible chance of success. But we must interminably challenge ourselves, if we are to achieve our dreams.

As an industry manager, executive recruiter, recruiting and sales trainer, event speaker, and as VP of a nationwide system of recruitment offices, the author has seen most every aspect of the hiring process from both the internal and external view as the decision-maker, the decision-influencer, and as the objective observer. This varied insight is what provides the clarity you will find in this book.

"Trust and have faith in yourself. Work and develop your abilities as a Self-Recruiter, and never shy away from the most difficult and unappetizing pieces, and you could end up in the place you might never have expected: the top."

John Crant